COORDINATING STUDENT AFFAIRS
DIVISIONAL ASSESSMENT

Coordinating Student Affairs Divisional Assessment

A Practical Guide

Edited by
**Kimberly Yousey-Elsener, Erin M. Bentrim, and
Gavin W. Henning**

Foreword by
Larry D. Roper

A JOINT PUBLICATION OF

STERLING, VIRGINIA

Published by Stylus Publishing, LLC.
22883 Quicksilver Drive
Sterling, Virginia 20166-2102

Library of Congress Cataloging-in-Publication-Data
Names: Yousey-Elsener, Kimberly, editor.
Title: Coordinating student affairs divisional assessment : a practical guide
   / edited by Kimberly Yousey-Elsener, Erin Bentrim and Gavin Henning ;
   foreword by Larry D. Roper.
Description: First edition. | Sterling, Virginia : Stylus Publishing, LLC,
   2016. | Includes index.
Identifiers: LCCN 2015020689 |
   ISBN 9781620363287 (pbk. : alk. paper) |
   ISBN 9781620363270 (cloth : alk. paper) |
   ISBN 9781620363294 (library networkable e-edition) |
   ISBN 9781620363300 (consumer e-edition)
Subjects: LCSH: Student affairs services--United States--Evaluation. |
   Student affairs services--United States--Administration |
   Student affairs administrators--United States.
Classification: LCC LB2342.92 .C68 2016 | DDC 371.4--dc23 LC record available at
http://lccn.loc.gov/2015020689

13-digit ISBN: 978-1-62036-327-0 (cloth)
13-digit ISBN: 978-1-62036-328-7 (paper)
13-digit ISBN: 978-1-62036-329-4 (library networkable e-edition)
13-digit ISBN: 978-1-62036-330-0 (consumer e-edition)

Printed in the United States of America

All first editions printed on acid-free paper
that meets the American National Standards Institute
Z39-48 Standard.

Bulk Purchases

Quantity discounts are available for use in workshops and
for staff development.
Call 1-800-232-0223

First Edition, 2015

10 9 8 7 6 5 4 3 2

We would like to dedicate this book to the members of Student Affairs Assessment Leaders who by their questions, conversations, and insights provided the inspiration for this book.

Thank you to the authors of each chapter in this book. We appreciate your willingness to share your experiences and expertise in order to help others.

Rob Aaron
Dan Bureau
Michael Christakis
James R. Doyle
Becki Elkins
Justin Keen
Ellen S. Meents-DeCaigny
Darby Roberts
Larry D. Roper
Vicki L. Wise

Contents

Figures

Foreword

AFTER MORE THAN TWO decades of sporadic activity, the student affairs assessment movement is on the cusp of aligning into a congruent community of practice. Up to this point, the organization of student affairs assessment efforts could largely be described as uneven, random, and idiosyncratic. Fortunately, leadership has emerged from among professionals charged with leading student affairs division assessment efforts and from within student affairs professional associations to provide support, guidance, and professional visibility to student affairs assessment. For example, the Student Affairs Assessment Leaders (SAAL) provides a forum for those who coordinate student affairs assessment efforts to convene and discuss matters relevant to sustaining and improving their work. Professional engagement, such as that provided by SAAL, is essential to coalesceing student affairs assessment. Currently, student assessment practices range from outstanding collaboration on some campuses to virtual isolation on others. Efforts such as ACPA's Student Affairs Assessment Institute; ACPA's Commission for Assessment and Evaluation; the NASPA Assessment, Evaluation, and Research Knowledge Community; and NASPA's Assessment and Persistence Conference are examples of professional associations' stimulating efforts to build a robust assessment community and cultivate more effective practice in that arena.

These and similar efforts are likely to be extremely beneficial resources to those who have established division assessment programs and are at various stages of developing their systems, processes, and practices. However, for those who have not yet created an assessment position or embarked on a division assessment program, entering a conversation with those who are at an advanced level of assessment work may be daunting. Fortunately, *Coordinating Student Affairs Divisional Assessment* has been written to respond to that exact need.

Coordinating Student Affairs Divisional Assessment is a comprehensive A–Z guide to establishing, evolving, and sustaining a student affairs division assessment program. The authors offer a practical and professionally grounded model to inform and support successful leadership of student affairs assessment.

Typically, many student affairs assessment programs were established in response to an urgent need to address accountability expectations. As a result of this urgency, the person appointed to lead the assessment efforts was often thrust into the role, expected to produce meaningful data, and charged with galvanizing the division's energy to support assessment activity. Assessment leaders often found themselves struggling to make sense of the role and to determine how to garner the support needed to be successful. Too often the senior student affairs officer would rely on the assessment leader to not only perform the role of providing the needed assessment data but also do the work of integrating assessment into the culture of the division. Not surprisingly, more often than not, efforts to create a culture of assessment proved to be more challenging than either the assessment leader or senior student affairs officer anticipated.

The beauty and brilliance of *Coordinating Student Affairs Divisional Assessment* is in the aggregate design it offers to demystify student affairs assessment and make successful leadership accessible. The editors of this book draw from a diverse group of experienced scholars and practitioners to bring contemporary perspectives and expertise to the reader. In the process of providing a guide to coordinating division assessment, the authors also provide a dynamic model of leadership—they go beyond "how-to" to help the reader understand why certain approaches matter and the implications of leadership activities and behavior. Too often, assessment is approached as merely a task, when, in fact, it is a culture-transforming activity that should be embedded in the ethos of a student affairs division—this perspective resonates throughout *Coordinating Student Affairs Divisional Assessment*.

Each chapter of this book connects seamlessly with all the other chapters, which helps reinforce the understanding that assessment leadership is more than a series of isolated activities to check off and instead requires engagement in a broad set of integrated experiences and the ability to balance tasks, achievements, relationships, content-specific knowledge, and unanticipated events.

Coordinating Student Affairs Divisional Assessment provides critical guidance for the successful leadership of student affairs assessment on college and university campuses. It provides a mission-related context and sound theoretical frameworks to help leaders construct viable and successful assessment programs. This book is theoretical, philosophical, and practical. It offers a strong introduction to the need for student affairs assessment and guidance on how to successfully transform student affairs culture.

Coordinating Student Affairs Divisional Assessment is a guide to action. This book provides a thoughtful and well-articulated process for establishing an assessment program, strengthening the culture of assessment, and sustaining long-term success, while offering solidly grounded strategies throughout.

This book is a guide to student affairs cultural transformation, offering pathways for transforming relationships, organizational learning, systems, and processes. It offers a plan for strengthening the connection between student affairs and the missions of our institutions. Kimberly Yousey-Elsener, Erin M. Bentrim, and Gavin W. Henning have successfully provided a critically needed resource to advance the leadership of student affairs assessment. With deep respect for all the wonderful work being done by student affairs leaders throughout the United States and beyond to strengthen the community of practice in student affairs assessment, this book can serve as a unifying element in our conversations going forward regarding how to launch successful divisional student affairs assessment.

This book should be on the reading list of every senior student affairs officer, regardless of where his or her division is in implementation of its assessment program, as it not only offers a process for initiating an assessment program but also provides a guide for evaluating the successful functioning of programs. Data will continue to be crucial to the success and survival of student affairs, as will the successful stewardship of student affairs organizations and institutional resources. This book contributes greatly to our ability to have a positive and productive future.

Larry D. Roper
Professor
School of Language, Culture, and Society
Oregon State University

Preface

Erin M. Bentrim
Gavin W. Henning
Kimberly Yousey-Elsener

IN 1903, 18 DEANS of women (Conference of the Deans of Women of the Midwest; see www.personal.kent.edu/~jgerda/1903ConfTyped .pdf) gathered to discuss how to structure their work on their own campuses and to share ideas for meeting the challenges of a newly created and undefined position. None were officially trained in what was now their professional work, and all felt they could use a connection with colleagues who were also making their way through the burgeoning field. Assessment coordinators frequently discover themselves in a situation much like the early deans, who, with little personal experience, found themselves wearing many hats and taking responsiblity for a multitude of activities loosely grouped together. For many professionals, assessment falls under "other duties as assigned," but a growing trend is for divisions of student affairs to employ a full-time assessment coordinator.

Coordinating Student Affairs Divisional Assessment stems from that growing trend and more specifically from a number of requests on the Student Affairs Assessment Leaders (SAAL) electronic mailing list (studentaffairsassessment.org) related to starting an assessment position in student affairs, creating an office, and developing a culture of assessment for divisions of student affairs. Before looking at current trends, it is important to look at a brief history of two movements coming together. The first movement, the student affairs profession, had its roots in the early twentieth century, while the second movement, assessment in higher education, started to take shape in the 1980s. It is important to understand the context of both of these movements to operationalize these frameworks in student affairs assessment work today.

Student Affairs Profession

The student affairs profession has a rich, diverse heritage. Although the titles, responsibilities, and organizational structures may have changed, many overarching principles have endured. As LeBaron Russell Briggs at Harvard and Alice Freeman Palmer at the University of Chicago approached uncharted territory as two of the earliest deans, their focus was on assisting student populations in a manner not previously seen on campuses. Granted, the initial impetus for creating such positions was out of administrative necessity as faculty were no longer willing to engage in administrative duties such as student conduct and residential oversight. Yet the value of these early positions was becoming increasingly apparent, and the rationale for providing students with these types of support services began to shift. What emerged eventually became and remains today the significant philosophical underpinning that guides the student affairs profession.

The major philosophical construct that shaped the work of student affairs, even prior to the American Council on Education's (1973) *Student Personnel Point of View,* is the stance that students are not purely academic creatures consisting of an array of purely cognitive functions. Rather, each student should be recognized as unique and complex, and his or her development should be considered holistically (American Council on Education, 1937). This idea of the "whole student" is clearly visible in other noteworthy documents, including *The Future of Student Affairs* (Miller & Prince, 1976) and *Learning Reconsidered* (Keeling, 2004).

Historically, the idea that student affairs services should explicitly champion the academic mission of the institution has been somewhat controversial. However, recent discussions on redefining the role of student affairs on college campuses reveal a clear trend toward additional emphasis on an academic model. The concept of partnerships is a significant focal point of several of the profession's more recent foundational documents, such as *Powerful Partnerships* (American Association for Higher Education, College Student Educators International, & National Association of Student Personnel Administrators, 1998), *Learning Reconsidered* (Keeling, 2004), and *Learning Reconsidered 2* (Keeling, 2006). Student affairs and academic affairs should be in an integrated, collaborative partnership within the framework of institutional mission and strategic planning.

In other words, the curricular and cocurricular (formerly extracurricular) become a single lens through which to view the education of students, or student learning. This theoretical paradigm has tremendous implications for higher education and student learning. If we are to form successful alliances and collaborations with academic affairs, then it is imperative that we can speak competently as educators and easily show the effectiveness and impact of our presence within the partnership on a range of measures such as student academic success, retention, persistence, and graduation rates. To understand the rise of assessment in student affairs, the discussion must begin with assessment in higher education in general.

Assessment in Higher Education

Although using assessment for understanding an individual's level of achievement or growth has been a practice as long as there has been teaching and learning, assessment as a movement in higher education can be traced to the early 1980s when the First National Conference on Assessment in Higher Education was held (Ewell, 2002). At that time, assessment was beginning to build on the foundation created by researchers in the areas of student learning, retention and student behaviors, program evaluations, and curriculum approaches related to mastery learning (Ewell, 2002).

Momentum for the movement picked up in the 1980s as calls for accountability in higher education grew louder from state governments (National Governors Association, 1986) and the federal government (National Commission of Excellence in Education, 1983). In the 1990s regional accreditation agencies gained more influence and began driving many institutional assessment efforts (Bresciani, Moore Gardner, & Hickmott, 2009).

During these decades one of the many debates was around the definition of *assessment*. While a definitive definition that fits all needs and disciplines has still not quite been realized, Ewell (2002) described three broad categories (or camps) that most assessment falls within:

1. Individual assessment is used to determine an individual's progress and provide feedback so that goals can be reached. This

is familiar to most of us through classroom assessment such as tests, papers, essays, projects, and so on, which are typically used for grading purposes as well as outside the classroom in things such as student staff evaluation feedback or diagnostic tests used in career services.

2. Large-scale assessment is used to benchmark or track a university or unit's performance, usually in the name of accountability.

3. Program assessment is used to gather evidence in order to improve student learning, programs, or services.

The focus of assessment in the 1990s shifted to establishing and measuring learning outcomes as outcomes became the emphasis of regional accreditation (Bresciani et al., 2009). When compliance was separated from the self-study process in regional accreditation process in the 2000s, focus shifted largely to teaching and learning. The focus of assessment had been in the academic areas where learning was taking place, but as higher education administrators realized that learning also happens outside the classroom, the profession of student affairs evolved and gathered speed around the call to facilitate student learning, assess quality, and use assessment to help define and improve the work being done with students outside the classroom.

Student Affairs Assessment

The merging of these two movements—the emergence of assessment in higher education and the evolution of the student affairs profession—have combined to create a submovement of student affairs assessment practice. During the past decade this professional practice has grown to adapt to internal priorities for data and information as well as external pressures, such as the demand from students, parents, and legislators for proof of outcomes and value in addition to accountability measures that show students are learning what they should be learning. Regional accrediting agencies continue to add to external pressures as they expand their scope of assessing student learning and institutional effectiveness beyond the classroom to the institution as a whole. A result of higher education recognizing the importance of these growing demands is the impetus to create assessment units within divisions of student affairs with the specific responsibility to measure and evaluate the impact of programs and services on students and their contribution to student success.

The history of student affairs assessment is perhaps the shortest and briefest of all these movements. The Council for the Advancement of Standards in Higher Education (CAS) was formed in 1979 (CAS, 2012). It created a set of national standards that are used to assess the quality of and guide practice in the student affairs profession. The first set of standards was published in 1986 and standards have been revised and created since (CAS, 2014). In the mid-1990s, publications such as Upcraft and Schuh's (1996) *Assessment in Student Affairs: A Guide for Practitioners* first acknowledged and addressed the specific needs of practitioners conducting assessment in student affairs. In 1999, Gary Malaney edited a *New Directions in Student Services* issue entitled "Student Affairs Research, Evaluation, and Assessment: Structure and Practice in an Era of Change," which identified the types of assessment work being done by student affairs assessment offices. As the movement continued to expand, by the mid-2000s there was a growing demand on student affairs professional organizations to provide some frameworks around professional development related to student affairs assessment. These frameworks—ACPA's *ASK Standards* (College Student Educators International [ACPA], 2006) and NASPA's *Assessment Education Framework* (Student Affairs Administrators in Higher Education [NASPA], 2009)—became foundational documents that were used to create specific professional development offerings at the national and local levels.

These foundational publications met the initial need for widespread professional development and learning opportunities for student affairs professionals conducting assessment at the program or departmental levels. But as demand for data and information increased and the sophistication needed to coordinate efforts grew, more campuses began to see the value in appointing assessment coordinators to guide and support assessment practice within an entire division. These positions take many different shapes and forms: some are full-time positions with individual or multiperson offices; others are part of a multifaceted leadership role (often at the association vice president level); and still others are part-time efforts being led by doctoral students, higher education faculty, or other professionals. No matter what the position may "look like" on any particular campus, for the purposes of this publication they are defined as the *assessment coordinators for the division of student affairs.*

The creation of this role is new to student affairs with few examples, and individuals filling them frequently find themselves in an in-between world. They are often not considered "student affairs practitioners" in the traditional sense of the phrase, while at the same time they are usually viewed as coming from the "outside" by colleagues doing similar work in institutional research and academic assessment offices. Like those who pioneered the higher education assessment movement and student affairs profession movements, these practitioners often have to pave a path on a campus where they are the only person doing this type of assessment work. This new and unique role within the field of student affairs created an additional need for professional support that is currently being served by SAAL (studentaffairsassessment.org), the NASPA Assessment, Evaluation, and Research Knowledge Community (www.naspa.org/constituent-groups/kcs/assessment-evaluation-and -research), and the ACPA Commission for Assessment and Evaluation (www.myacpa.org/commae). Each of these groups continues to develop resources, programming, and networking opportunities for professionals seeking to lead assessment efforts.

As more institutions create these positions, there is a greater demand for resources created specifically for student affairs assessment coordinators that address common challenges and issues related to creating assessment systems, cultures, and structures. It is with this demand in mind that the editors set out to create this publication. This book is framed with the understanding that anyone entering a student affairs assessment coordinator position already has the following foundational skill sets:

1. Knowledge in student development theory and the application of such theory
2. A strong background in "data literacy," meaning assessment skills such as writing outcomes; the ability to design data collection instruments; and the skills to interpret, analyze, and present data to statistical and nonstatistical audiences

If a new coordinator finds either of these skill sets challenging, he or she should work first to hone and build these proficiencies before taking on some of the larger concepts included in this book.

Having established these skill sets, the task of leading assessment efforts can begin. Keep in mind that unless the coordinator is fortunate enough to have a multiperson office where some of the day-to-day assessment tasks, such as data analysis and interpretation, can be done by someone else, one of the consistent challenges for coordinators is serving a multitude of constituencies, often with competing priorities, while shifting between thinking "big picture" and "small picture." The chapters in this book serve as a guide to creating systems and structures that help balance these challenges, while also moving a division forward in assessment practice.

Book Overview

Chapter 1, "Tenet One: Building Capacity in Student Affairs Assessment: Roles of Student Affairs Assessment Coordinators," illuminates the different functions required of an assessment coordinator through the lens of capacity building. It defines these roles through six key tasks:

1. Creating an evidence-based culture and attitude
2. Developing talent and managing knowledge
3. Generating and disseminating knowledge
4. Planning strategically
5. Engaging and collaborating with stakeholders
6. Administrating technology

The remainder of this publication seeks to explore each of these elements in detail as well as overarching areas such as ethics and politics.

Chapter 2, "Tenet Two: Cultivating a Culture of Assessment," examines what it means to develop and create a culture of assessment and then provides several strategies one can use in the role of assessment coordinator in order to establish, enhance, and build a culture within the organization.

Chapter 3, "Tenet Three: Developing Infrastructure for Student Affairs Assessment Practices," discusses the importance of building infrastructure within the assessment coordinator's office and organization. Whether or not the office is made up of one or many people, taking time to strategically plan and position assessment efforts helps ensure the office's overall success. This chapter explores how assessment can both fit into and enhance the overall infrastructure of the division of student affairs and discusses how to increase intentionality and support divisional goals.

Chapter 4, "Tenet Four: Leading Logistical and Administrative Tasks in Student Affairs," considers elements such as where an assessment office falls in the organizational structure, how it is funded, and other logistical matters. The chapter focuses on three key areas—organizational structure, strategic resource planning, and project planning—and discusses techniques and resources related to establishing a strong administrative function to support assessment efforts.

Technology is used to help advance assessment efforts while also creating effective and efficient systems for collecting, analyzing, and reporting data. Chapter 5, "Tenet Five: Using Technology to Advance Assessment," focuses solely on using technology to assist in assessment efforts, provides an overview of the role of technology, describes the different types of technology available for use in an assessment office, and presents information on how to select technology based on the various options available.

Chapter 6, "Tenet Six: Building Talent and Increasing Assessment Knowledge," explores the significant role of building assessment skills and talent throughout the organization. This chapter provides links to resources from campuses throughout the United States that have created formal mechanisms such as assessment glossaries and toolboxes as well as informal mechanisms such as workshops and boot camps. It also discusses the importance of informal educational moments to develop the skills and abilities throughout all levels of an organization.

Most divisions of student affairs build their infrastructure around key elements such as resource allocation and decision making. Chapter 7, "Tenet Seven: Connecting Assessment to Planning, Decision Making, and Resource Allocation," focuses on incorporating assessment into these foundational efforts through the creation of an integrated assessment model. In addition, the chapter provides resources on how to use this integrated model in measuring progress toward strategic planning goals and in processes related to decision making and resource allocation.

The volume concludes with three chapters that examine overarching topics that are essential to the role of assessment coordinator. Chapter 8, "Tenet Eight: Cultivating Ethical Assessment Practice," examines the role of the assessment coordinator in leading and maintaining ethical standards related to data collection, storage, and sharing for the division.

Added to ethical considerations is the reality that the assessment coordinator functions in a dynamic political environment where data and information can be powerful tools. Chapter 9, "Tenet Nine: Navigating Politics," examines political situations often encountered by assessment professionals.

And, finally, Chapter 10, "Tenet Ten: 'Other Duties as Assigned,'" adds a little humor while discussing some "other duties" that many assessment coordinators find themselves doing as part of their role. Through sharing examples contributed by many different assessment coordinators, this chapter discusses the benefits of taking on additional responsibilities while also providing advice on how to ensure that these additional duties do not overshadow the meaningful assessment work that needs to be completed.

The goal of this publication is to provide a resource for those starting assessment offices or those newly appointed to student affairs assessment coordinator positions. Each chapter is designed to explain key concepts and discuss important considerations, as well as provide tools and resources to get started.

References

American Association for Higher Education, College Student Educators International, National Association of Student Personnel Administrators. (1998). *Powerful partnerships: A shared responsibility for learning.* Retrieved from www .aahe.org/assessment/joint.htm.

American Council on Education. (1937). *The student personnel point of view.* American Council on Education Studies, Series 1, Vol. 1, No. 3. Washington, DC: American Council on Education.

Bresciani, M. J., Moore Gardner, M., & Hickmott, J. (2009). *Demonstrating student success: A practical guide to outcomes-based assessment of learning and development in student affairs.* Sterling, VA: Stylus.

College Student Educators International (ACPA). (2006). *ASK standards: Content standards for student affairs practitioners and scholars.* Retrieved from www.myacpa.org/ask-standards-booklet.

Council for the Advancement of Standards in Higher Education. (2012). *CAS professional standards for higher education* (8th ed.). Washington, DC: Council for the Advancement of Standards in Higher Education.

Council for the Advancement of Standards in Higher Education. (2014). *CAS history.* Retrieved from www.cas.edu/history.

Ewell, P. T. (2002). An emerging scholarship: A brief history of assessment. In T. W. Banta (Ed.). *Building a scholarship of assessment* (pp. 3–26). San Francisco, CA: Jossey-Bass.

Keeling, R. P. (Ed.). (2004). *Learning reconsidered: A campus-wide focus on the student experience.* Washington, DC: National Association of Student Personnel Administrators and American College Personnel Association.

Keeling, R. P. (Ed.). (2006). *Learning reconsidered 2: Implementing a campus-wide focus on the student experience.* Washington, DC: National Association of Student Personnel Administrators and American College Personnel Association.

Malaney, G. (Ed.). (1999). *Student affairs research, evaluation, and assessment: Structure and practice in an era of change. New Directions for Student Services, Number 85.* San Francisco, CA: Jossey-Bass.

Miller, T. K., & Prince, J. S. (1976). *The future of student affairs.* San Francisco, CA: Jossey-Bass.

National Commission of Excellence in Education. (1983). *A nation at risk: The imperative for educational reform.* Washington, DC: U.S. Government Printing Office.

National Governors Association. (1986). *Time for results: The Governors 1991 report on education.* Washington, DC: National Governor's Association, Center for Policy Research and Analysis.

Student Affairs Administrators in Higher Education (NASPA). (2009). *Assessment education framework.* Retrieved from www.northwestern.edu/studentaffairs/assessment/media/pdfs/FrameworkBrochure-Dec09.pdf.

Upcraft, M. L., & Schuh, J. H. (1996). *Assessment in student affairs: A guide for practitioners.* San Francisco, CA: Jossey-Bass.

1

Tenet One: Building Capacity in Student Affairs Assessment:

Roles of Student Affairs Assessment Coordinators

Erin M. Bentrim
Gavin W. Henning

C*APACITY BUILDING* is defined most simply as the intentional and planned development of an increase in skills or knowledge or allowing organizations or individuals to fulfill their mission in the most effective and productive manner. It is considered an ongoing and evidence-based process that results in measurable and sustainable actions. Capacity building is often associated with a conceptual framework that is quite similar to what is required of an assessment coordinator. When viewed through this framework, the argument can be made that the primary role of an assessment coordinator is to be a capacity builder—one who builds the assessment knowledge and skills capacity for a division of student affairs and ultimately allows staff members in the division to perform their own assessments. Being a capacity builder requires the assessment coordinator to play a number of roles, including the following:

- Evidence-based culture and attitude creator
- Talent development and knowledge manager
- Knowledge generator and disseminator
- Strategic planner
- Stakeholder engager and collaborator
- Technology administrator

This chapter focuses on further defining the roles that stem from the overarching umbrella of an assessment coordinator as a capacity

1

builder. In addition, the later chapters in this book provide additional detailed examination and discussion.

History of Capacity Building

The concept of capacity building grew out of the theory of organizational development. Kurt Lewin, the founder of social psychology, was also a pioneer in the field of group dynamics and organizational development. It was through his work that psychologists realized organizational structures and processes influence worker behaviors and that feedback was a powerful tool for success (Lewin, 1947). Beckhard (1969) built on Lewin's work and defined *organizational development* as a process by which organizations plan for success from the bottom up. He believed that expanding the level of knowledge and creating feelings of ownership in people on a team would allow organizations to manage change successfully and improve overall performance.

Over time, the term *capacity building* evolved to refer to a very specific type of organizational development. In the 1960s and 1970s, it was primarily applied to the idea of expanding the self-help abilities of individuals living in rural communities and gradually to those individuals in power in developing countries. The focus was on the human resource issues. However, because of the shifting political landscape of the 1980s, the idea of sustainable capacity building became popular. Capacity building is no longer seen as a "matter of building institutional person-power to the point where there is an adequate skills base" (Centre for Higher Education Transformation, 2002, p. 1). Instead, capacity building should be viewed as a more complex web of relationships that focuses on building up the complete organization rather than the individuals who comprise the organization. In other words, if the organization does not have a vision, values, and an infrastructure in place, then the number of skilled individuals available does not matter.

In the late 1990s, it became popular to apply capacity-building theory to higher education and other nonprofits. For the most part, nonprofit organizations were the early adopters of capacity building as a developmental approach. However, as cultural and political landscapes continued to shift and public calls for accountability grew louder, colleges and universities began responding as well. Not to be underestimated is the impact of the work of Paulo Freire on the concept of organizational capacity building in higher education.

Freire's (1970) most influential work argued against the idea of the traditional "banking" education model where a hierarchy of knowledge (teacher as expert) exists. Although Freire's criticisms against tabula rasa were not new, he updated the concept and expanded it into a theory of dialogue between equals that had a global impact on the discourse of race, class, and social justice in education. This philosophy became known as *critical pedagogy* and called for a participatory relationship between teaching and learning.

Because of the amalgamation of capacity building over the past 20 years, plus the fact that it is a relatively new concept, some confusion and ambiguity remain regarding *capacity building's* precise definition, how to operationalize it, and how to identify a common framework. For the purposes of this text, consider that assessment coordinators are primarily capacity builders through an innovative lens of critical pedagogy with an organizational development strategy adapted from Beckhard's (1969) consultant scheme. In other words, the assessment coordinator is a professional who provides individuals with the tools and education to make assessment a participatory process.

Because of the complexity of the position, the assessment coordinator must be ready to shift gears quickly and seamlessly. While the diversity of tasks and roles is exciting, it also introduces challenges. Within a one-hour meeting, the coordinator may need act as director, educator, conflict manager, and statistician. The purpose of this first chapter is to discuss the most common roles an assessment coordinator may need to assume.

The variety of positions and responsibilities seems to be endless. Often, roles depend on the size of the institution, the size of the assessment office, and the organizational structure of the assessment office. An assessment system at the division level is different from an assessment system at the institution level, at the department level, and so forth. However, a common core of responsibilities exists across all levels.

Elements of Building Capacity in Student Affairs Assessment

Because of these varying roles, assessment coordinators often find themselves in a position with a much larger scope than simply collecting, analyzing, and reporting on data. In order for assessment efforts to be successful and for the assessment coordinator position to be sustainable, the coordinator needs to think of himself or herself as one who is building capacity throughout the division or unit. This section applies the concepts used with organizational capacity building through the lens of student affairs assessment.

Evidence-Based Culture and Attitude Creator

First, an organizational attitude must be established. Starting with an environmental scan is often recommended. One of the roles of a coordinator as capacity builder is to create an *evidence-based culture and attitude*. It is imperative that this culture is intentionally developed vertically (from top leadership to lower tiers) and horizontally (across and between divisions). Without a systemic approach, assessment happens only in silos or pockets and can defeat the most well-intentioned professional.

Building a culture of assessment and establishing the organizational attitude can be arduous at times. Indeed, it may be one of the most difficult tasks a coordinator faces if the division is not curious, introspective, or willing to invest the time and effort needed. Surprisingly, the coordinator's skills in relationship building and motivating play larger roles during this time than during the actual assessment experience.

In their book *Switch: How to Change Things When Change Is Hard*, Chip Heath and Dan Heath (2010) discussed three ways to change culture. The authors made the case for appealing to logic (explain why assessment is important and necessary), appealing to emotion (alleviate the fear and anxiety around the process), and making it easy to change (provide clear direction within a positive environment that ensures success).

Talent Development and Knowledge Manager

Second, capacity building could be defined as *talent development* or *knowledge management* of staff members. Staff members must have appropriate assessment skills and knowledge to develop an evidence-based culture. Each unit in the division has different levels of comprehension and skills. All these needs must be met and nurtured by the assessment coordinator. Coordinators spend a lot of time educating, coaching, and serving as professional development providers. The venues for such educational opportunities depend on the desires and needs of the division, so a needs assessment is recommended before designing an assessment curriculum. Often, professional organizations offer workshops, webinars, and other resources to assist in this process. It is wise to take advantage of such opportunities and offer them to others within the division.

It is critical to begin with a set of intended learning outcomes for staff related to assessment skills and knowledge. The ACPA/NASPA assessment, evaluation, and research (AER) competencies provide the foundation for these outcomes. In addition, rubrics created by ACPA's Commission for Assessment and Evaluation have been developed for the 2010 version competencies. The dimensions in the rubric provide content areas around which educational opportunities can be created. The rubrics also provide an assessment tool that can be used as a needs assessment, baseline assessment, or an evaluation tool for individuals or learning activities. The rubrics can be adapted in many ways to meet a variety of needs.

Once the content areas are identified, the curriculum can be developed. Keeping the theory and process of engaging adult learners (andragogy) in mind, multiple delivery methods should be used. These methods could be group focused and centered on workshops or conferences or on external consultants who provide workshops, webinars, and reading groups. The offerings might even include individual-focused activities, such as reading, consultations, or certificate programs such as the Association of College and University Housing Officers-International's Certificate in Housing Assessment program. The goal is to provide many different options to meet everyone's learning styles.

An effective option is a version of an "assessment boot camp." This is a single or multiday intensive assessment training program designed to quickly bring all staff members to the same basic level of knowledge for consistency and offer further educational opportunities designed to increase skills and capacities. This event has multiple interactive and engaging sessions. This not only increases staff members' skills and knowledge, but also serves as a motivational tool. This option can be a productive way to kick off a new academic year. Using the assessment camp as a springboard, additional professional development opportunities can then be developed to address various staff members' needs.

After the coordinator helps build the basic capacity of staff, the staff members themselves can then begin to provide the training to others. Assessment showcases or poster sessions are superb ways to highlight assessment activities occurring across the division, provide recognition for staff doing assessment, and empower others. Staff members who participated remarked that by teaching their assessment project, they ultimately expanded their own assessment skills.

Knowledge Generator and Data Disseminator

Third, the coordinator is responsible for not only the development and management of the knowledge of others, but also the coordination of the process for *knowledge generation* across unit, division, and institution levels. Since this frequently takes the shape of survey administration, that will be the focus here.

Assessment coordinators may coordinate and administer large-scale surveys for various constituents. The process for administration of large-scale surveys is quite complex, and it requires meticulous attention to detail. The coordinator must attend to sampling methods, physical administration of the survey, and the cleaning of data prior to analysis.

Management of these large-scale surveys does not cease when administration is completed. *Data dissemination* and *reporting* are as complex as administration. Assessment coordinators may work individually or in tandem with their institutional research colleagues to analyze the data and draft the report. Analysis and report writing can take a great deal of time, especially if administrators expect in-depth analyses and comprehensive reports. One report is often insufficient because each audience needs different information in different formats.

Another responsibility related to data collection is the coordination of surveys by staff across the division. As surveys continue to be the primary form of data collection, it is incumbent upon the assessment coordinator to help manage these surveys so students are not oversurveyed, and multiple surveys asking similar questions are not distributed.

Some divisions are moving to centralized processes for survey approval and scheduling. The survey-approval process serves four purposes. First, it helps ensure that the surveys being distributed are of acceptable quality and rigor. This review and approval process can be completed by the assessment coordinator or by a trained assessment committee, which helps relieve some of the coordinator's burden. A second purpose for an approval process is similar to the work done by institutional review boards; the reviewer can ensure that participants' rights are protected. Third, the review process can ensure that the same data are not collected in multiple surveys and help realize opportunities to combine similar surveys so that only one is administered. The fourth purpose of a centralized approval process is to schedule survey distribution so that survey administration does not overlap or compete with other institutional activities or priorities. Coordinated data collection helps improve the quality of the data collected and reduces the burden on students.

Strategic Planner

Fourth, a vision and strategy should be developed. The assessment coordinator may be the facilitator of strategic planning. Strategic planning is a complex form of assessment. Bryson (2011) defined *strategic planning* as a "deliberative, disciplined approach to producing fundamental decisions and actions that shape and guide what an organization (or other entity) is, what it does, and why" (pp. 7–8). Most strategic plans employ the following stepwise process:

1. Identify a set of priorities or goals that are aligned with the mission and vision of the organization.
2. Establish initiatives to achieve these priorities.
3. Determine the metrics by which initiatives will be measured.
4. Collect data.
5. Create an action plan.

Assessment planning follows a similar design. Suskie (2009) outlined the assessment process for measuring learning outcomes. She states that the assessment process begins with explicit, intended learning outcomes that must be aligned with the institutional mission and purpose. Once these outcomes are established, learning strategies to foster these outcomes are developed. Data are then collected and analyzed to determine if the outcomes were achieved, and, finally, data are used to improve the learning process.

Given the close relationship between strategic planning and assessment, responsibility for strategic planning is often given to the assessment coordinator, likely in addition to establishing the system to track and monitor progress. This means the assessment coordinator needs to work collaboratively with the senior leadership to develop not only content but also the infrastructure that is needed to implement, sustain, and monitor the plan to fruition.

Implementing and monitoring a strategic plan can be a full-time job. Formative and summative data should be collected to track progress toward strategic goal achievement so adjustments can be made along the way. Juggling multiple strategies with multiple action steps for each goal, this process can get complex. Thus, a system for managing the strategic plan is crucial. Fortunately, many software tools such as Compliance Assist!, Taskstream, and WEAVEonline can provide the technological platform to assist with this management. However, project management skills are required to gather the data at the defined intervals and make decisions regarding progress.

Stakeholder Engager and Collaborator

Fifth, capacity building involves the ability to *manage stakeholder (internal and external) engagement and collaborate across boundaries* (e.g., academic affairs, trustees, senior leadership, and other administrative units not related to student affairs). An assessment coordinator must be perceptive to the needs of multiple stakeholders, provide leadership across boundaries, and, simultaneously, adeptly communicate and explain the impact and consequences of results and other assessment knowledge. Simply put, the coordinator must translate and "tell the story" to multiple audiences. Being able to translate terms, concepts, and statistical language for different audiences is inherent in this aspect.

Staff members in offices such as financial aid, bursar, admissions, and even health services may not envision themselves as educators or appreciate how their interactions with students are applicable to learning and retention. An assessment coordinator should help make this connection explicit. Service delivery transactions can be integrated into educational conversations with students.

Storytelling is complex, as there are many audiences for the stories and each story requires different information, a different approach, or a different format depending on the audience. The story for senior administrators looks different than the story for students or the story for community members surrounding the college or institution.

Assessment is as much about telling stories as it is about evaluation. Assessment can be used to tell different types of stories, including what student affairs staff members do, the value of the work, the impact of the work, and, most importantly, the effect on student learning and development. In addition, information distribution must be adapted for various stakeholders.

Technology Administrator

Sixth, an assessment coordinator might find himself or herself tasked with *technology administration*. This might come in the form of managing, recommending, or developing systems (both commercial and in house), and acting as support staff and data retriever. It is often the responsibility of the assessment coordinator to manage the data-tracking technology used in the division. This responsibility requires a coordinator comfortable with technology who can readily learn how to use numerous tools. In other words, the coordinator must be proficient in creating and sharing knowledge through appropriate tools.

Serving as the technology manager often necessitates an additional role related to data retrieval. While senior leadership may have access to data housed in the software, frequently only the coordinator has the knowledge and capability to access the data quickly and easily. Because of this skill, the assessment coordinator often fields requests for data from across the division and institution. Developing a policy and process for distribution and use of data by staff is critical. This policy must be consistent with institutional and federal policies protecting student identification of data. Restrictions should be set for the distribution and use of data related to sensitive topics (e.g., sexual assault, alcohol and drug use, etc.).

Summary

The work of student affairs assessment coordinators is ultimately related to helping staff in the division build capacity to perform assessment. Under the umbrella of capacity building, coordinators must fulfill a number of roles, including evidence-based culture and attitude creator, talent development and knowledge manager, knowledge generator and data disseminator, strategic planner, stakeholder engager and collaborator, and technology administrator. Effectively managing all these roles is a complex task that requires a diverse skill set and a many resources.

References

Beckhard, R. (1969). *Organization development: Strategies and models.* Reading, MA: Addison-Wesley.

Bryson, J. (2011). *Strategic planning for public and nonprofit organizations: A guide to strengthening and sustaining organizational achievement* (4th ed.). San Francisco, CA: Jossey-Bass.

Centre for Higher Education Transformation. (2002). *Capacity building initiatives in higher education.* Retrieved from www.google.com/url?sa=t&rct=j&q=&esrc=s&source=web&cd=2&ved=0CCkQFjAB&url=http%3A%2F%2Fchet.org.za%2Fdownload%2Ffile%2Ffid%2F199&ei=uPkNVIDoNbWMsQSHmIGYCw&usg=AFQjCNHCTMy8pzBQZpKc-Mxg5XSwDWVmAw&sig2=L3KjE7s5VIPLWe8IEtte_w&bvm=bv.74649129,d.cWc

Freire, P. (1970). *Pedagogy of the oppressed.* New York, NY: Herder and Herder.

Heath, C., & Heath, D. (2011). *Switch: How to change things when change is hard.* New York, NY: Broadway Books.

Lewin, K. (1947). Frontiers of group dynamics: Concept, method, and reality in social science, social equilibria and social change. *Human Relations, 1*(1), 5–41.

Suskie, L. (2009). *Assessing student learning: A common sense guide.* San Francisco, CA: Jossey-Bass.

2 Tenet Two: Cultivating a Culture of Assessment

Gavin W. Henning

An ASSESSMENT coordinator in a division of student affairs has numerous roles and responsibilities, but one of the most important tasks is cultivating a culture of assessment. Before cultivation can be discussed, a culture of assessment must be explained. Goffee and Jones (1998) defined *culture* as a set of shared values, symbols, behaviors, and assumptions. In the context of assessment, a culture is related to people, behaviors, and data. Culp (2012) defined a *culture of evidence* as:

> a commitment among student affairs professionals to use hard data to show how the programs they offer, the processes they implement, and the services they provide are effective and contribute significantly to an institution's ability to reach its stated goals and fulfill its mission. (p. 5)

Another definition of *culture of assessment* is that it is a set of pervasive actions and behaviors by staff across an organization (e.g., unit, division, etc.), focusing on the use of data in decision making regarding the accountability and improvement of programs and services. The use of data to demonstrate the impact of programs and services is not sufficient. Data must also be used to identify ways the programs and services can be continually improved.

Characteristics

After defining a *culture of assessment*, it is helpful to identify the characteristics of such a culture. What does a culture of assessment look like? For divisions with cultures of assessment, assessment is not just performed for program review or during the regional reaccreditation self-study process. It is performed on an ongoing basis with participation from multiple stakeholders throughout the division. In other words, assessment is ingrained in the everyday practice throughout the division. Assessment is not simply an activity; it is a state of mind and being, practiced unconsciously as part of the daily routine (Henning, 2013a). Because of this pervasiveness, assessment functions must be the responsibility of many people. While there may be a coordinator and/or assessment committee to lead and support the efforts for the division, assessment is the responsibility of all staff members seeking to improve their own programs and services.

When assessment is distributed throughout a division as part of the daily routine, it follows that data collection also involves a variety of techniques not isolated to surveys, focus groups, and interviews. Strong cultures of assessment evolve to incorporate multiple methods of data collection for viewing any one topic in order to provide the most complete picture of the program or service available. Having a culture of assessment also means that once the data are collected and analyzed, they are used to "tell the story" of the unit. Information is packaged in a format for distribution to stakeholders and typically differs depending on the stakeholders as each group is compelled by different reporting formats and has needs for different types of data. Finally, and most importantly, data are used to "close the loop" to enact improvement. This implies that data are being used to effect change and are more than a list of recommendations at the end of an assessment report. Once the loop is closed, the process begins anew.

Strategies

Cultivating a culture of assessment across a division of student affairs is easier said than done. Often, student affairs staff members don't believe they have the skills or knowledge to perform assessment. Others feel they have limited time for assessment activities. Bresciani (2006) suggested the following obstacles: professionals do not understand the value of assessment, other staff members may fear the process, and assessment activities are not appropriately allocated resources.

Now that a *culture of assessment* has been defined and characterized, how exactly do student affairs assessment coordinators cultivate a culture of assessment? Suskie (2009) outlined the following four keys to fostering a culture of assessment:

- Value campus culture and history.
- Respect and empower people, especially faculty.
- Value innovation and risk taking, especially in improving teaching.
- Value assessment efforts especially by supporting them with appropriate resources and infrastructure and using the results to inform important decisions on important goals. (p. 70)

Schuh (2013) outlined 10 characteristics of institutions with cultures of assessment.

1. There is recognition that assessment is a commitment not only of accountability to stakeholders but also to continual improvement.
2. There is a commitment to student affairs practice (restlessness) and improvement.
3. Institutions are self-critical.
4. Data-driven decision making is used.
5. Institution-wide assessments are made.
6. Multiple forms of assessment contribute to a culture of assessment.
7. Learning outcomes are identified and measured.
8. While someone needs to be in charge, all student affairs staff members should pitch in when it comes to assessment.
9. Results are communicated and acted on.
10. Discretionary resources are used to seed assessment projects.

3x5 Plan for Cultivating a Culture of Assessment

Building on the work of previous assessment scholars, the 3x5 model for cultivating a culture of assessment incorporates some of those strategies and others in a three-pronged model. The prongs focus on three main domains of building a culture of assessment—foundation, implementation, and support. Each domain has five components. A division that has a foundation for assessment is mission centered, goal grounded, outcome directed, culture specific, and literature based. Regarding implementation, assessment is focused on the dual purposes of assessment—accountability and improvement—embedded in daily practice as a collaborative, transparent, ongoing, and never-ending effort. Support for cultures of assessment include a vocal and unyielding leader, a champion, infrastructure, continual skill and knowledge development, and robust resources. Each domain and component is described in detail in the following sections.

Foundation for Assessment

Regardless of what is being built, be it a house or skyscraper, the foundation must come first. The same is true for a culture of assessment. Without a strong foundation, the culture cannot be appropriately developed or sustained over time.

Mission Centered

The mission should be the base for all work within a division of student affairs. Bryson (2011) stated that a "mission . . . clarifies an organization's purpose, or why it should be doing what it does" (p. 127). He went on to explain that the mission should answer six questions if it is going to be a declaration of organizational purpose. Those questions can be paraphrased as follows:

1. Who are we?
2. What needs do we exist to address?
3. What do we do to respond to these needs?
4. How should we respond to our stakeholders?

5. What are our philosophies, values, and culture?
6. What makes us unique?

The mission derived from the answers to these questions provides the foundation for the organization's work.

Just as the divisional mission should guide the overall work of the division, it should also provide direction for assessment activities. Assessment helps support the mission by providing evidence documenting the extent to which the mission is being addressed and how mission-related work can better support the strategic direction of the division. While there may be times for assessment activities not related to the mission, it is prudent to allocate assessment resources for programs and services that directly support the mission. As the assessment coordinator develops the short-term and long-term items on the assessment agenda, the divisional mission should be at the forefront of that decision-making process.

Goal Grounded

A culture of assessment cannot, however, be cultivated simply by centering work on the mission; it must also be goal grounded. Missions undergird the work of an office, department, or entire division. But, as such, missions are somewhat broad. The mission must be honed into goals that provide further illumination of how work must be done. Goals are guideposts or beacons, giving direction and illuminating the end result (Henning, 2013b). Goals provide the "destination postcard" for what that end result looks like.

It is often helpful to embed the goals in a strategic plan, thus providing a structure for intentional goal achievement. However, strategic plans do not include all goals an office, department, or division strives to achieve. Regardless of the fact that goals may or may not be part of a strategic plan, the goals should provide an additional layer in the foundation for a culture of assessment. Without these beacons, staff members are not clear on what is to be achieved.

Outcome Directed

Outcomes are more specific, measureable elements of goals. There are often multiple outcomes for each goal. Henning (2013c) defined three types of outcomes: *operational, learning,* and *program. Operational outcomes*, also called *service* or *administrative outcomes*, as well as *targets*, are metrics that document how well operational aspects of a program or service are functioning, but they do not document learning or the overall impact of a program or activity. The focus is on process, not end results. Examples of operational outcomes include the number of programs in a residence hall during an academic year, the number of contact hours in the counseling center, the satisfaction rates for facilities in a fitness center, or the average number of students who frequent the student union from 10:00 p.m. to 12:00 a.m. on Friday nights during a certain month (Henning, 2013b). *Learning outcomes* are the knowledge, skills, attitudes, and habits of mind that students take with them from a learning experience (Suskie, 2009). Finally, *program outcomes* are aggregate effects of a program, service, or intervention. Some examples of program outcomes may include a targeted reduction in the binge-drinking rate on campus, an increase in the number of students who receive the seasonal flu vaccine, a decrease in damage billing in a residence hall, an increase in first- to second-year retention rates, or an increase in the percentage of underrepresented students graduating in five years (Henning, 2013b). The focus of program outcomes is on impact, not process.

There are many ways in which outcomes are advantageous.

- They help provide direction at the beginning of the activity. A specific product or result is conceptualized and agreed on.
- Outcomes keep all staff members consistent so that each person is collaborating for the same conclusion.
- The specificity of the outcomes provides clarity for what exactly to assess.
- Once the end result is known, the process for identifying strategies to achieve the effect is easier.
- Once the members know the end result and identify strategies for achieving that result, a unit can then determine the resources needed to implement those strategies.
- For learning outcomes, the statements themselves assist students in articulating to others what they have learned (or at least should have learned).
- Because outcomes provide a clear end point, the process for fostering outcomes is focused. The outcomes can be revisited to ensure strategies are on track and allow for midstream readjustment.

- Explicitly stating outcomes provides critical information to constituent groups regarding an office's intent, role, and purposes. As many stakeholders are unaware of the value of student affairs units, this transparency is essential.

Regardless of the type of outcome being addressed, outcome statements should be "SMARRT." There are different words for each letter depending on which author you read, but the letters often stand for *specific*, *measureable*, *attainable*, *results oriented*, *relevant*, and *time*-bound (Henning, 2013c).

For an outcome to provide adequate direction for staff, it must be specific. The outcome must be crystal clear and free from misinterpretation. For example, a division of student affairs may develop an outcome similar to the following: as a result of the alcohol education programs on campus during the 2015–2016 academic year, the binge-drinking rate on campus will decrease by 5% for that year. This outcome is specific. It identifies what is intended to decrease the binge rate (alcohol education programs). The term *binge-drinking rate* has been operationalized in the literature so it can be measured, and there is a specific time frame for when the decrease should occur.

Outcomes should be assessed, and as such they need to be measureable. With a target of a 5% reduction, the binge rate in 2015–2016 can be easily measured and compared with previous years to determine if it has decreased.

Although this may seem obvious, the outcome must be attainable or achievable. It is difficult to set a department's or division's staff members' sights on an outcome that cannot be obtained. If it cannot be obtained, the outcome cannot be measured, and the process of achieving the outcome may be futile. A 5% reduction is aggressive since literature suggests reducing the binge rate is difficult, but this outcome is attainable. A reduction of 25% on most campuses would be impossible within a one-year time span.

All outcomes should be results oriented. The focus of the outcome should be on what is completed or achieved rather than what goes into helping achieve the end result. In this example, the focus is on the reduction in binge rate. It is not on how much money will be spent, how much staff time will be used, or even on the number of initiatives that will be implemented. These items are important to consider, but they are not the focus of the outcome itself.

The outcome should also be relevant. Given the ongoing concern of alcohol abuse on college campuses and the secondary effects of this abuse, an outcome to decrease the binge rate would be relevant. Often, relevance means that the outcome is aligned with missions, goals, or strategic priorities.

Finally, the outcome should be time bound. It is essential to identify when the change is expected to occur. In this case it is at the end of the 2015–2016 academic year. The time frame helps determine both an action plan for achieving the outcome and a time frame for measurement. If the outcome was to occur over a five-year period, different strategies and different measurement times might be considered. Regardless of specifics, when considering outcomes, ensure that each one is SMARRT.

Culture Specific

Culture is defined as an organization's shared values, symbols, behaviors, and assumptions (Goffee & Jones, 1998). In other words, it is "the way we do things here" (Martin, 2006). While similarities abound, no two organizational cultures are identical. Organizational structure influences and is influenced by organizational culture. Sandeen (2001) identified the following factors that influence student affairs organizations: institutional mission and culture, professional background of the student affairs staff, student characteristics, presidents and senior academic officers, academic organizations, financial resources, technology, and legislation and court decisions. Additional attributes that influence culture include size and prestige. The culture for a division of student affairs is influenced by institutional characteristics as well as the division's approach to student affairs. These approaches are student services, student development, and student learning (Manning, Kinzie, & Schuh, 2006). A culture of assessment must be situated in the larger organizational culture, and alignment between these cultures must occur to successfully cultivate a culture of assessment.

When cultivating a culture of assessment there are a few components of organizational culture to be cognizant of, including the following: the value of assessment, direction of authority, centralization, transparency, and integration with academic affairs. Consider the value placed on assessment in the division. Cultures that place a high value on assessment have an already established infrastructure, assessment is a part of multiple conversations on various levels, and resources are allocated toward these efforts. Often, a chief student affairs officer who values assessment and is trying to create a culture around this value creates an assessment coordinator position, but because the elements of this culture do not exist yet the position lacks impact.

Another characteristic to consider is the direction of authority. For staff members who have worked in different divisions or for different vice presidents or deans, the culture can vary from hierarchical to flat or somewhere in between. This approach to authority has implications for how the culture of assessment is developed. In a hierarchical structure, the chief student affairs officer may want to be involved in all (or most) decisions regarding assessment. As such the culture is imbued with the values of that individual. In a more egalitarian structure, the culture has the ability to take on the values of the entire division because the coordinator can involve many individuals in the cultivation of the culture.

Centralization is another component of culture to consider. This is similar to the direction of authority; a centralized culture is characterized by the power in one individual, whereas a decentralized culture has power radiating from multiple individuals. Centralized cultures have assessment functions centered on one person or office, and processes occur in a more controlled fashion. In decentralized cultures, assessment happens in multiple offices across the division, but not necessarily in a coordinated fashion. It is important to note that not all divisions with an assessment coordinator or office operate in a centralized culture as there are many decentralized institutions with a full-time assessment coordinator. As a result, many processes created by these coordinators either look highly centralized (e.g., divisional planning and reporting templates) or highly individualized by department or unit.

Transparency is discussed in greater detail later, but it should be touched on briefly here. Some organizational cultures are more transparent than others. This is dependent, to an extent, on the control of the institution, as public institutions are required by state and federal law to share more data than private institutions. The level of transparency has implications for how assessment is implemented and the extent to which the data are shared internally and externally.

A final structural component of culture to consider is the level of integration with academic affairs. Some divisions of student affairs are separate from academic affairs. This integration could result from both divisions reporting to the provost or vice president for academic affairs. At some institutions, the integration is only related to assessment functions, as there may be one assessment director for the entire institution. The culture of assessment must be cultivated in a way that corresponds with each institution's unique academic affairs culture. In some cases the assessment directives may come from academic affairs, while in other institutions they come from student affairs administrators. It is essential to understand the institutional and divisional cultures to cultivate a culture of assessment in student affairs.

Literature Based

Student affairs as a field is becoming more professionalized, and a key factor in that professionalization is a growing literature base. All of this literature provides building blocks for a foundation of practice. Student affairs educators can no longer develop programs and services based solely on anecdotes and personal experiences. While those resources provide some useful information, student affairs work must be based on systematized collection, analysis, and synthesis of data and development of theory. The use of theory and data for program development is even more important in this era of limited and declining resources. It is critical that we integrate current literature into our assessment practice to inform program development, data collection, and analysis.

Just as programs and services must have foundations in theory and research, assessment must also have the same foundation. Theory must be integrated with assessment practice. In cultivating a culture of assessment, the assessment coordinator must continually compel staff to perform a literature review (even a small one) before embarking on an assessment project. Research can help staff hone outcomes, provide direction for strategies to achieve those outcomes, and help contextualize assessment results so that the loop can be properly closed and resources can be used most effectively and efficiently. There may be instances where research does not exist for a particular issue or problem. In these situations, it is important to take the time to develop a conceptual framework that can provide an intentionally considered context for the project.

Consider a new program developed to help students increase their moral development as they proceed through a student conduct process. For this program, it would be essential to understand the various theories of college student moral development. All theories may not be used or useful as the foundation of the program because of their distinct characters, but they all should be considered and one should be chosen. The theory can be used to help establish appropriate outcomes for students, identify probable strategies for achieving those outcomes, and assist with interpretation of the assessment data.

Implementation of Assessment

Once the foundation is set for assessment, the focus should turn to how assessment should be implemented across the division. The following five components outline considerations for implementation.

Accountability and Improvement

Accountability and improvement are the two overarching purposes for assessment. Accountability demonstrates with evidence that "we do what we say we do" and the "extent to which we do what we say." In other words, accountability is the demonstration of goals and outcomes achievement. Of course, this assumes that there are goals and outcomes to start with. Accountability was recently catapulted to the top of the national higher education agenda with *A Test of Leadership: Charting the Future of U.S. Higher Education* (Spellings Commission, 2006), a report commissioned by U.S. Secretary of Education Margaret Spellings. This report decried higher education and was a rally call for holding colleges and universities, individually and collectively, responsible for student learning. Since then, initiatives such as the Voluntary System of Accountability (www .voluntarysystem.org), Voluntary Framework of Accountability for Community Colleges (www.vfa.aacc.nche.edu), the University and College Accountability Network (www.ucan-network.org), and the College Scorecard (www.whitehouse.gov/issues/education /higher-education/college-score-card) launched by President Obama in his 2013 State of the Union address have been developed to address this issue.

It is important to note that the rise of external accountability is partly due to the lack of internal accountability. Particularly in student affairs, administrators and educators were not doing an adequate job telling the story of their impact on student learning and the student experience. The assumption was that constituents on campus understood the work student affairs educators performed. In the absence of internal accountability, external accountability filled the void. With the increased focus on external accountability in the national higher education conversation, the second grand purpose of assessment, improvement, has been somewhat drowned out. In addition to demonstrated achievement of goals and outcomes, assessment should be used to identify opportunities for improvement moving forward. The assessment loop is closed when those improvements are made.

The challenge is that the data needed to demonstrate accountability are often not the same data needed to identify opportunities for improvement. If an aim is to demonstrate goal or outcome achievement, the focus is on gathering summative data for accountability, while formative data are needed for improvement. Formative assessment questions include the following: What percentage of students graduated in five years? What was the alcohol binge rate in the past academic year? What did students learn by participating in the orientation program? The data needed to answer these "what" questions are summative in nature and are different from the data needed to determine the "how" questions for improvement. If outcomes such as these are achieved, data need to be gathered to help understand how they can be achieved. For instance, how to increase the five-year graduation rate, how to decrease the percentage of students who binge drink, and how to ensure that students learn what we want them to learn during orientation are different concerns with different answers. While the data are different for accountability and improvement, there is additional tension between these concepts.

In 2009, Peter Ewell revisited the tension between accountability and improvement that he discussed in 1987. In this more recent paper titled *Assessment, Accountability, and Improvement: Revisiting the Tension*, Ewell discussed the challenges between these two grand purposes. He stated that the incentives for each purpose are different.

Accountability requires the entity held accountable to demonstrate, with evidence, conformity with an established standard of process or outcome. The associated incentive for that entity is to look as good as possible, regardless of the underlying performance. Improvement, in turn, entails an opposite set of incentives. Deficiencies in performance must be faithfully detected and reported so that they can be acted upon. (2009, p. 7)

The task is reconciling these two purposes. Sometimes both can be addressed in the same assessment project; sometimes they cannot. It is up to the assessment coordinator to navigate and balance these competing purposes.

Embedded

For many staff members, assessment is a burden—an additional task added to an already heaping plate of responsibilities that keeps getting higher and higher. Assessment coordinators strive to transform this mind-set. Assessment should not be seen as an additional task, a singular activity that is performed at the end of a program or a service. We should no longer be sending out surveys a week after a program. Rather, we should be identifying ways to integrate assessment into the activity, program, or service, making it a seamless component.

In the book *Switch: How to Change Things When Change Is Hard,* authors Chip and Dan Heath (2010) pointed out that one way to make change happen is to shape the path, making it easy for people to change behaviors. Within that category, one specific strategy is to "build habits." By this, the Heath brothers meant that habits need to be encouraged to make behavior automatic. In other words, coordinators should develop ways to do assessment so assessment is no longer an activity, but a state of mind. Embedding assessment into the activity itself is a way to build habits. Methods such as one-minute papers, muddiest point, focused listing, and others provide evidence regarding what students know or have learned, and the assessment activities themselves also foster learning. These methods create "reflection traps," permitting the student to take a few minutes to process or reflect on what he or she has learned. With some creativity, these methods can even be scaled up for large groups of students. Assessment methods that provide assessment evidence and foster learning are ideal as they serve two purposes at once.

While it may be easier to embed assessment methods into learning activities, they can also be embedded into service activities. Point-of-service assessments, brief highly targeted assessments done immediately before, during, or after a service is provided, are useful tools to achieve this goal. To better understand sleeping behavior on campus, rather than filling out a survey they receive in their campus e-mail, students could complete a one- or two-question minisurvey when they visit the health center. Upon check in, students can complete the questions on a tablet in the waiting area or on a small piece of paper, then place the paper in a locked box similar to a comment box. Although the sample may not be representative, this is an easy way to embed assessment into another activity. This approach is likely just as valid as a campus survey that has a 25% response rate.

Embedded assessments are usually easier, more interesting, and more useful than traditional after-event assessments.

Collaborative

As John Schuh (2013) stated, "While someone needs to be in charge, all student affairs staff members should pitch in when it comes to assessment" (p. 94). It is easy for staff members, and even division leaders, to overly rely on the assessment coordinator to do all the assessment in the division. The coordinator has the formal responsibility and the expertise and enjoys the work. However, depending on one person to do all or most of the assessment in the division is not sustainable over the long term. In addition, a culture of assessment cannot evolve if everyone is not investing in performing assessment.

It is essential that expectations are established for all staff members to engage in assessment even if there is a divisional coordinator and/or departmental point people. These expectations need to come from the leadership. There also should be opportunities created that bring people together to discuss the assessment that they are doing. These activities reinforce the expectations. Another strategy is to identify goals and outcomes that transcend multiple offices and have staff members from those offices discuss how those goals and outcomes can be assessed collaboratively. A final strategy that institutionalizes these expectations is to integrate assessment responsibilities into every job description and make assessment a component of annual performance evaluations. It is important to note that the focus on the evaluations is simply engaging in assessment, not on the results themselves. If staff members feel as though their personal performance is based on the results of the assessments, they are less likely to perform assessment for fear of the impact on their evaluation.

Transparent

It is easy to be transparent with assessment data when the information demonstrates programs are successful and students are learning what they are expected to learn. Transparency is not so easy when the results show the opposite information. It is difficult to show warts. However, good, bad, or ugly, it is critical to be transparent with assessment results and assessment processes. There are a number of reasons for this; Schuh (2009) described two. First, students and parents are becoming consumers of higher education assessment data. They are beginning to question the return on investment of college tuition and fees. Second, the federal government is nudging institutions to share more data, and soon the nudge will turn into policy.

Aside from the external factors influencing transparency, there are internal reasons, as well. The more student affairs professionals are open about assessment processes and data, the more credibility they garner. With greater transparency, assessment is no longer seen as some political process that takes place in a darkly lit room to produce data that spin the "right" story. By sharing both positive and negative assessment data, professionals can tell the "whole" story. More importantly, when stakeholders see how the data are being used to create change, they are more supportive of assessment and more willing to be a participant in assessment processes as they know there will be some larger benefit to their participation.

Ongoing and Never Ending

Many readers will recall the Energizer Bunny commercials. In those commercials, Energizer batteries were put into a pink toy bunny, after which it was able to walk and play a bass drum simultaneously. The tagline was that Energizer batteries "keep going and going and going."

That is the same way to think about assessment. Assessment cannot be "one and done." It cannot be episodic when a program needs to be defended, nor will an 18-month cycle every 10 years in preparation of a reaccreditation visit suffice. Assessment has to be ongoing. This does not mean that everything has to be assessed all the time—that is just not possible. But it is important to develop an assessment plan for the department or division so that there is a clear blueprint for how assessment is done and integrated into the work of the unit. Again, assessment cannot be just an activity. It has to be a state of mind.

Support for Assessment

The final domain in cultivating a culture of assessment is providing support for assessment efforts. Even with a strong foundation and solid principles for implementation, a culture of assessment is not sustainable without internal and external support.

Vocal and Unyielding Leadership

Vocal and unyielding leadership is a critical component to building and maintaining a culture of assessment. Often, the prime mover for a culture of assessment is a divisional leader who values assessment inherently and is not motivated by external accountability. This leadership is a strong cornerstone in creating a culture of assessment. Leaders of cultures of assessment understand the importance of data to inform decision making, and thus they set expectations regarding the use of data (Yousey-Elsener, 2014).

The leader needs to continually vocalize the importance of assessment and its benefits while supporting those comments with examples and evidence regarding how assessment has been used to tell the division's story and make improvements. Simply saying assessment is important is not enough, no matter how often it is proselytized. The benefits need to be substantiated to convince others that assessment is a valuable process in which to engage.

The leader also has to be unyielding as there will undoubtedly be pushback. Staff members often make comments such as the following: "I don't have time to do assessment." "How am I supposed to fit this in among my million other responsibilities?" "I don't know how to do assessment." "This will take away from my direct work with students." "Can't we just hire a work-study student to do this?" Rather than shunning these responses, an effective leader must understand that these comments often come from staff members who care about their work and students but are frightened, insecure in their ability, and overworked. Thus, there is some validity to their responses even if they seem petty. The leader cannot give in to these reactions but must seek to understand them to provide the support and resources needed to convert these detractors into advocates of assessment. This takes perseverance and compassion by the divisional leader and assessment coordinator.

Championed Across the Division

A vocal, unyielding leader is a necessary component of support when building and maintaining a culture of assessment, but a leader alone is not sufficient. A culture of assessment needs a champion. This is a person who motivates people when assessment gets difficult. The champion keeps an eye on the "big picture" of assessment in the division, sees how all the parts fit together, and campaigns for resources to continue to develop the culture of assessment. Often, the champion is not the divisional leader, as the chief student affairs officer does not have the time to attend to all these assessment-related responsibilities. For institutions with a student affairs assessment coordinator, this person serves as the champion. The associate or assistant vice president (if he or she has a portfolio that includes assessment) plays this role for institutions that do not have a coordinator.

Strong Infrastructure

Building an infrastructure to support assessment efforts is one of the most critical components of sustaining a culture of assessment. Established policies and practices provide the scaffolding that supports assessment efforts by the staff. Heath and Heath (2010) defined this as "tweaking the environment" or shaping the path to make it easy to change behavior. In their book *Switch: How to Change Things When Change Is Hard*, Heath and Heath (2010) point out that changing the environment helps change behavior. To support this notion, they discuss the research that suggests that by simply using a smaller plate, people will consume less food.

Thus, in order to encourage assessment, processes and policies should be developed that make it easier to perform assessment. The development of an assessment coordinator position is a key element of the infrastructure to develop and maintain a culture of assessment. Another common tool is the development of templates for curricular mapping, assessment reports, and the like. These templates make it easier for staff to engage in assessment activities. Some institutions revise their annual reporting process by creating quarterly reports that focus primarily on assessment data. Still other divisions invest in software systems that track and report assessment information. The assessment champion has to scan the environment and understand the divisional and institutional culture to determine what infrastructure needs to be built, and the divisional leader needs to finance that infrastructure.

Continual Skill and Knowledge Development

As stated earlier in the discussion of collaboration, one person cannot and should not perform all assessment in a division. To involve all staff members in assessment efforts they need the skills, knowledge, and confidence to do assessment themselves.

Good starting points in building these attributes are the ACPA/NASPA professional competencies (www.myacpa.org/professional-competencies). One of the competencies is focused on assessment, evaluation, and research (AER). The AER competency provides a framework for creating a professional development curriculum that can be used to help staff members cultivate the necessary skills and knowledge to perform assessment.

A rubric has also been developed for the 2010 AER competency (www.myacpa.org/files/professional-comp-rubricspdf) (Yousey-Elsener, n.d.). This rubric can be used as a needs assessment or an evaluation of a professional development activity. Perhaps more usefully, the dimensions of the ACPA/NASPA AER competency identified in the rubric could serve as domains for skill and knowledge development. The dimensions include the following: terms and concepts, value of assessment, purpose, design, data collection, analysis, interpreting results, reporting, use of results, politics, creating systems, and ethics.

Once the content areas for capacity building have been defined, delivery methods need to be identified. These methods could include on-campus workshops, readings, and discussions; attendance at assessment programs at the NASPA and/or ACPA annual conventions; and participation in national assessment events such as the ACPA Student Affairs Assessment Institute or the NASPA Assessment and Persistence Conference. Divisions may hire a consultant to provide the training, or staff members may choose to use the AER competency to develop their own professional development plan. There can be many components to an intentional plan to build the assessment capacity of staff.

Robust Resources

Resources to support assessment can take many forms. Resources can include providing financial support for staff to attend conferences or hiring an external consultant to provide training. Release time to work on assessment projects or reallocation of responsibilities freeing up workloads for assessment practices can also be a form of resources. Access to books, literature, and other readings are also resources to sustain assessment practice.

Divisional leaders and champions need to decide what types of resources are required and which are financially feasible. The choice of resources depends on the needs of the organization and the funding available. Leaders and champions should visit the NASPA and ACPA webpages to view professional development events offered by each association. They may also want to visit www.assessment conferences.com to view upcoming conferences. Champions may also wish to build an assessment library for staff. If so, some texts to consider can be found at the end of this chapter (see "Further Resources" and "References").

Tips for Cultivating a Culture of Assessment

Armed with a framework for cultivating a culture of assessment, where does one begin to actually develop this culture? Following are tips for next steps.

Develop a Support Network

One of the first steps is to develop a support network. Being an assessment coordinator is a lonely position at most institutions since these are one-person offices. To counteract this challenge, join groups such as Student Affairs Assessment Leaders, the NASPA AER Knowledge Community, or the ACPA Commission for Assessment and Evaluation. In these groups, assessment coordinators find people in similar positions who can provide support and guidance.

Attend Conference Sessions

Being an assessment coordinator requires individual skill and knowledge development. One should consider attending assessment conferences or identifying assessment sessions at national conventions to develop the skills and knowledge needed to build a culture of evidence.

Develop a Resource Clearinghouse

A resource clearinghouse is useful for both assessment coordinators and their staff. This clearinghouse may contain assessment articles, a list of assessment books (and maybe the books themselves), conference presentation materials, and a list of helpful online resources. SAAL has a growing repository of assessment resources that members have shared. The coordinator should make time each week, no matter how difficult that may seem, to review resources in the clearinghouse. In this role, ongoing professional development is key.

Build Relationships

Building relationships is an essential step in developing a culture of assessment. Coordinators need to foster trust with staff members, allowing them to embrace the change process in creating this culture and to connect with the coordinator as a change leader. It is also critical for the coordinator to nurture relationships with divisional leaders, as these leaders can help support the change process.

Conclusion

Cultivating a culture of assessment is not an easy task. Change is difficult. The status quo is comfortable. However, the benefits foster change, and building a culture of assessment is well worth the effort. A culture of assessment helps staff members more effectively deliver services and foster learning. Resources in all forms—money, space, and staff time—are used more efficiently. Priorities are easier to determine, and the division or department can more successfully tell the story of how it adds value to the institution by helping students learn and develop. This chapter provides the blueprint for developing a culture of assessment. The remaining chapters provide more information on the tools one can use to help establish this culture.

Further Resources

Web Resources

Association for Higher Education Effectiveness
www.ahee.org
Association for the Assessment of Learning in Higher Education
www.aalhe.org
Council for the Advancement of Standards in Higher Education
www.cas.edu
Internet Resources for Higher Education Outcomes Assessment
www2.acs.ncsu.edu/UPA/archives/assmt/resource.htm
National Institute for Learning Outcomes Assessment
www.learningoutcomeassessment.org
Student Affairs Assessment Leaders
www.studentaffairsassessment.org

Text Resources

Allen, K. R., Elkins, B., Henning, G. W., Bayless, L. A., & Gordon, T. W. (2013). *Accreditation and the role of the student affairs professional.* Washington, DC: ACPA-College Student Educators International. Retrieved from www2.myacpa .org/publications

American College Personnel Association (ACPA). (2007). ASK *standards: Assessment skills and knowledge content standards for student affairs practitioners and scholars*. Washington, DC: American College Personnel Association.

Angelo, T., & Cross, K. (1993). *Class assessment techniques: A handbook for college teachers*. San Francisco, CA: Jossey-Bass.

Bresciani, M. J. (2011). *Making assessment meaningful: What new student affairs professionals and those new to assessment need to know*. NILOA Assessment Brief: Student Affairs. Urbana: University for Illinois and Indiana University, National Institute for Learning Outcomes Assessment.

Bresciani, M. J., Moore Gardner, M., & Hickmott, J. (2010). *Demonstrating student success: A practical guide to outcomes-based assessment of learning and development in student affairs*. Sterling, VA: Stylus.

Bresciani, M. J., Zelna, C. L., & Anderson, J. A. (2004). *Assessing student learning and development: A handbook for practitioners*. Washington, DC: National Association of Student Personnel Administrators.

Council for the Advancement of Standards in Higher Education. (2012). *Professional standards in higher education* (8th ed.). Washington, DC: Council for the Advancement of Standards in Higher Education.

Culp, M. M., & Dungy, G. J. (Eds.). (2012). *Building a culture of evidence in student affairs: A guide for leaders and practitioners*. Washington, DC: National Association of Student Personnel Administrators.

Keeling, R. P. (Ed.). (2004). *Learning reconsidered. A campus-wide focus on the student experience*. Washington, DC: National Association of Student Personnel Administrators & American College Personnel Association.

Keeling, R. P. (Ed). (2006). *Learning reconsidered 2: A practical guide to implementing a campus-wide focus on the student experience*. Washington, DC: Human Kinetics.

Keeling, R. P., Wall, A. F., Underhile, R., & Dungy, G. J. (2008). *Assessment reconsidered*. Washington, DC: International Center for Student Success and Institutional Accountability.

Maki, P. L. (2004). *Assessing for learning: Building a sustainable commitment across the institution*. Sterling, VA: Stylus.

Schuh, J. (Ed.). (2013). Selected contemporary issues in assessment. In J. Schuh (Ed.), *New directions in student services 2013* (p. 142). San Francisco, CA: Jossey-Bass.

Schuh, J. M., & Associates. (2008). *Assessment methods for student affairs*. San Francisco, CA: Jossey-Bass.

Schuh, J. H., & Gansemer-Topf, A. M. (2010). *The role of student affairs in student learning assessment*. NILOA Occasional Paper No. 7. Urbana: University of Illinois and Indiana University, National Institute for Learning Outcomes Assessment.

Schuh, J. M., Upcraft, M. L., & Associates. (2001). *Assessment practice in student affairs: An applications manual*. San Francisco, CA: Jossey-Bass.

Suskie, L. A. (2009). *Assessing student learning: A common sense guide* (2nd ed.). San Francisco, CA: Jossey-Bass.

Timm, D. M., Davis Barham, J., McKinney, J., & Knerr, A. R. (2013). *Assessment in practice: A companion guide to the ASK standards*. Washington, DC: ACPA-College Student Educators International. Retrieved from www2.myacpa.org/publications

Upcraft, M. L., & Schuh, J. H. (1996). *Assessment in student affairs: A guide for practitioners*. San Francisco, CA: Jossey-Bass.

References

Bresciani, M. (2006). *Outcomes-based academic and co-curricular program review: A compilation of institutional good practices*. Sterling, VA: Stylus.

Bryson, J. M. (2011). *Strategic planning for public and nonprofit organizations: A guide to strengthening and sustaining organizational achievement* (3rd ed.). San Francisco, CA: Jossey-Bass.

Culp, M. M. (2012). *Building a culture of evidence in student affairs: A guide for leaders and practitioners*. Washington, DC: National Association of Student Personnel Administrators.

Ewell, P. (2009). *Assessment, accountability, and improvement: Revisiting the tension*. Champaign, IL: National Institute for Learning Outcomes Assessment.

Goffee, R., & Jones, G. (1998). *The character of a corporation*. New York: Harper Business.

Heath, C., & Heath, D. (2010). *Switch: How to change things when change is hard*. New York: Broadway Books.

Henning, G. (2013a). Assessment isn't an activity. It's a state of mind. In *2nd annual international forum on student affairs*. Monterrey, Mexico.

Henning, G. W. (2013b). Documenting student learning and institutional effectiveness. In K. R. Allen, B. Elkins, G. W. Henning, L. A. Bayless, & T. W. Gordon (Eds.), *Accreditation and the role of the student affairs educator* (pp. 6–13). Washington, DC: American College Personnel Association.

Henning, G. W. (2013c). Get SMART: Developing outcomes. In *Systematizing assessment across student affairs*. Portland, OR: Academic Impressions.

Manning, K., Kinzie, J., & Schuh, J. (2006). *One size does not fit all*. New York, NY: Routledge.

Martin, M. J. (2006). That's the way we do things around here: An overview of organizational culture. *Electronic Journal of Academic and Special Librarianship*, 7(1). Retrieved from http://southernlibrarianship.icaap.org/content/v07n01/martin_m01.htm

Sandeen, A. (2001). Organizing student affairs divisions. In R. B. Winston Jr., D. G. Creamer, T. K. Miller & Associates, *The professional student affairs administrator* (pp. 181–209). New York, NY: Routledge.

Schuh, J. (2009). Looking into the future of assessment: Some ideas and musings. In J. Schuh (Ed.), *Assessment methods for student affairs* (pp. 231–248). San Francisco, CA: Jossey-Bass.

Schuh, J. (2013). Developing a culture of assessment in student affairs. In J. Schuh (Ed.), *New directions in student services* (pp. 89–98). San Francisco, CA: Jossey-Bass.

Spelling, M. (2006). *A test of leadership: Charting the future of U.S. higher education.* Retrieved from https://www2.ed.gov/about/bdscomm/list/hiedfuture/reports/final-report.pdf

Suskie, L. (2009). *Assessing student learning: A common sense guide.* San Francisco: Jossey-Bass.

Yousey-Elsener, K. (2014). Using data to inform decision making. In *University of Buffalo Supervisor's Learning Forum.* Buffalo, NY.

Yousey-Elsener, K. (n.d.). *Professional competency areas for student affairs practitioners: Rubrics for professional development.* Washington, DC: American College Personnel Association.

3 Tenet Three: Developing Infrastructure for Student Affairs Assessment Practices

Michael Christakis
Dan Bureau

CONSIDER THE National Highway System (NHS)—a series of highways throughout the United States that serves major airports, seaports, railway stations, and other strategic transport facilities. The NHS is the largest highway system in the world. Most U.S. residents have used this vast, interconnected system of highways going to work, on a family vacation, or on a business trip. Thanks to the NHS, you get from point A to point B quickly and efficiently with (some level of) certainty.

Let's consider how the first author of this chapter might use the system to meet up in the hometown of the second author. In order to get from Albany to Memphis, he has at least two options. He could fly from Albany to Memphis; it would take about four hours and cost about $400 round-trip. Or he could drive from Albany to Memphis on I-90 (west) and I-72 (south); it would take about 17.5 hours and cost about $340 in gas money. There are several more options, of course—any number of local "county roads" are available as is public transportation (e.g., bus, cab). He could patch together a series of rail systems and take the train; he could even walk, run, or bike from Albany to Memphis. Some questions to be considered include the following: When does he need to arrive in Memphis? How much money does he have in his budget to get there? Are there other tasks between Albany and Memphis that could be accomplished on the trip? There are numerous considerations that must be examined as he launches this important journey from one place to another.

This fleeting example of infrastructure is provided to set the stage for a discussion on how divisions of student affairs benefit from a robust infrastructure that facilitates efficient, systemic, and reliable assessment. In fact, there are all kinds of systems and processes that influence higher education and student affairs—we just might not think of them collectively as the infrastructure of our work. *Infrastructure* in student affairs assessment can be defined as the systems established and resources provided to accomplish assessment priorities. Once systems are in place and appropriate resources are allocated, infrastructure emerges as a framework for student affairs assessment practice.

Previous chapters in this volume provide strategies for leading divisional efforts to build assessment capacity. Once capacity increases, a division of student affairs can develop a culture of assessment. Such a culture sets up expectations that staff members will use evidence to make decisions and develop plans that take existing practices and create strategies for improvement. One aspect of building a culture of assessment is designing infrastructure. This chapter explains the importance of infrastructure, key elements of assessment infrastructure, and the benefits of using infrastructure to create processes needed to sustain assessment practices in a division of student affairs.

Why Assessment Infrastructure Is Important

Similar to a journey from Albany to Memphis, divisions of student affairs have and/or create plans and processes to realize goals within specific institutional contexts. Divisions of student affairs already have various types of infrastructure in place such as strategic plans, financial management systems, frameworks for ongoing professional development, policies and procedures for the safety and well-being of students, and so on. In most cases, student affairs professionals work within infrastructures that influence day-to-day operations and the student experience. If student affairs professionals believe that infrastructure matters when developing successful programs, resources, and services, then why would assessment be approached with any less intention?

The message that "assessment matters in student affairs" has been widely touted over the past decade via various publications (Bresciani, 2010; Collins & Roberts, 2012; Schuh & Gansemer-Topf, 2010), as well as by the ACPA and NASPA professional competencies (American College Personnel Association & National Association of Student Personnel Administrators, 2010). It is evident that the field of student affairs must incorporate assessment practices, and, therefore, the infrastructure to support such practices must be established.

Key Elements of Assessment Infrastructure

Establishing an assessment infrastructure ensures that assessment efforts are intentional, eliminates barriers by clearly stating expectations, and allows for better management of resources. The sections that follow discuss each of these elements and provides examples of how infrastructure can be built to best support quality assessment efforts.

Intentional Approaches

Going back to the metaphor of the NHS, consider travel without using this path: slow, winding, uncertain, and unpredictable. One would never start a trip from Albany to Memphis without some plan, so why start assessment without intention? As a map provides a sense of direction and intention, the use of infrastructure enables intentionality to guide student affairs assessment work.

Intentionality is defined as the process in which professionals use frameworks for good assessment practice. Frameworks come in various shapes and sizes; they might be a planning template, a set of goals or priorities, or external resources such as those provided by the Council for the Advancement of Standards (CAS) or the Association of American Colleges and Universities (AAC&U). In the case of CAS, which provides predetermined standards for diverse functional areas, intentionality comes about because the standards provide direction and guidance for what is expected in student affairs work.

No matter what framework is used, intentionality is created when assessment infrastructure provides a guide to determine priorities and act with purpose and intention. The infrastructure is essentially set up to ensure that the work is intentional.

Consider a division of student affairs at a large public research university that is seeking to be more intentional in how it contributes to the academic mission of the institution. Upon the assessment coordinator's recommendation, the vice president calls on unit heads to develop unit-specific learning outcome statements as part of the annual reporting process. This is not accomplished in a vacuum. Rather, unit heads are provided with a divisional student learning outcomes framework that espouses four broad learning domains and a series of more specific learning dimensions. The framework provides the theoretical infrastructure for the types of learning experiences units provide. Without this divisional infrastructure for learning outcomes development, units would be creating learning outcomes not expressly related to the division's broader learning aspirations and therefore might miss the opportunity to relate to the larger-picture efforts happening at the university.

Units cannot be expected to do assessment in isolation. Intentionality helps staff members understand why assessment matters and what frameworks, processes, and procedures are in place to help them fulfill assessment expectations. Using an intentional framework as part of the infrastructure provides units with clear expectations for how their work advances the division's and institution's efforts and therefore allows units to be better contributors in the assessment process.

Clarifying Functions and Expectations

An intentional framework helps guide units in their assessment work. Another key element is clarifying functions and expectations. Infrastructure should itself guide the assessment process from start to finish by focusing on specific tasks and expectations throughout a cycle. Many student affairs divisions use an assessment cycle or something similar (e.g., institutional or division assessment-planning timeline) (Collins & Roberts, 2012; Culp & Dungy, 2012). A simple version of the assessment cycle may be a good place to start. Versions such as the one in Figure 3.1 include only four components and may be more intuitive for staff:

1. Establish goals (have a plan).
2. Create or match with opportunities to reach goals (e.g., programs, services, learning opportunities).
3. Gather data (determine if the plan worked).
4. Use results (make improvements) (Suskie, 2009).

This piece of infrastructure helps capture the impact of student affairs, and staff members are better able to understand the expectations they contribute to desired results (Maki, 2004; Yousey, 2006).

While the cycle in Figure 3.1 is intuitive and easy to follow, sometimes more detail is needed to clarify each step along the way or to support training, reporting templates, and so on. The detailed assessment cycle (Figure 3.2), adopted widely by student affairs divisions nationally, is useful in detailing the steps associated with a comprehensive assessment process but may prove daunting for even the most seasoned assessment professional (Yousey, Elkins, & Timm, 2007). It is not unheard of for staff members to spend months upon months framing goals only to see the semester pass them by before they can actually administer an assessment to their students.

One role of an assessment coordinator is to determine what type of structure or assessment cycle works best within a specific culture

Figure 3.1   Simplified assessment cycle.

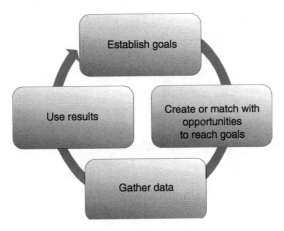

Figure 3.2   Detailed assessment cycle.

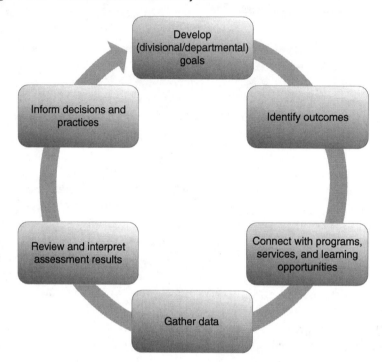

and context. Most coordinators prefer to create a cycle that uses language familiar to faculty and staff on their campus and provides enough steps to guide the process without being overwhelming. (Yousey-Elsener, 2013).

Table 3.1 identifies the various "stages" of both the detailed and simplified assessment cycles. Again, choosing a cycle that works within a specific context and culture is one of the most important aspects of creating a strong infrastructure. In addition to setting clear expectations related to the process of conducting assessment, it is also important to set clear timelines for each step of the assessment cycle. Adopting such an infrastructure helps staff members become clear on the processes in which they are participating. As this happens expectations are met, and staff members will most likely complete their programs' goals while advancing their divisions' and departments' broader goals. As such expectations are met, it is

Table 3.1   **Comparison of Detailed and Simplified Assessment Cycle**

Detailed Assessment Cycle	Simplified Assessment Cycle
1. Develop (divisional/departmental) goals.	1. Develop (program-level) outcomes.
2. Provide programs, services, and activities.	2. Develop strategies.
3. Develop assessment.	3. Gather data.
4. Gather data.	
5. Review assessment results.	4. Close the loop.
6. Inform decisions and practices.	

vital that staff members are given the resources needed to be successful. Another reason for developing infrastructure is to manage those resources.

Managing Resources

Let us return to the metaphor of a road map to explain managing resources as a rationale for student affairs assessment infrastructure. As a group departs for their road trip, they bring with them the appropriate resources to ensure the journey results in getting to the final destination: enough drivers, sufficient gas money, possibly a printed map or GPS, and memories each person brings about potential locations to stop for dinner or lodging. Similarly, in the context of student affairs infrastructure, professionals should take stock of what resources are at their disposal and determine when it is appropriate to expend such resources, particularly if they are limited. Still another reason for assessment infrastructure and systems is to identify processes to determine how fiscal, human, technological, and intellectual resources will be allocated.

> *Fiscal resources.* Whether in a budget-neutral or budget-rich environment, the allocation of fiscal resources is critical to ensuring divisions provide programs, resources, services, and activities that positively contribute to our students' experiences. Assessment can be an indicator of budget use and,

therefore, a source of data to inform budget decisions (Schuh, 2003). Accordingly, efforts should be made to inform staff of how assessment processes influence financial resource decisions (and vice versa). Few student affairs divisions are flush with the resources needed to meet all the needs of the students and stakeholders with whom we work. Having an assessment infrastructure and related systems can help us explain to staff how allocation of resources will be made: provide evidence that your programs support institutional goals, and you are more likely to receive the financial resources you need.

Human resources. Developing an infrastructure can explain the extent to which people conduct the work of assessment in a division of student affairs. As with financial resources, few divisions of student affairs have all the human resources they need (Dalton, 2003). For example, while residence life may have sufficient staff members to manage residence halls and address campus programming, an office such as disability resources may not have the human support it needs to meet student expectations and conduct assessment activities on top of expected position duties. Having an infrastructure for assessment practices can help staff members recognize how to incorporate assessment into practices regardless of the number of staff. Assessment infrastructure may require staff to be creative with human resources, such as involving campus partners on an advisory board that conducts assessment. Departmental leadership may have to reassign duties from one person to another (or eliminate less important duties) so that assessment of programs, resources, services, and activities can become a priority. Having an assessment infrastructure that is intentional and clearly articulated helps managers determine when assessment resources are needed and plan it into staffs' portfolios.

Technological resources. In this day and age, assessment processes require more than just the right human and fiscal resources. They are also dependent on good technology (Junco, 2014). Technology can be for the development of a process (e.g., a software platform that manages planning documents), the collection of data (e.g., tools that help with survey administration or data coding), and the promotion of data to tell the student affairs story (e.g., social media venues). Technology has become a vehicle to manage the infrastructures throughout student affairs. For example, strategic planning software allows for student affairs to monitor progress and the process by which social media becomes a platform that student affairs staff members use to market programs. Relative to assessment infrastructure, staff invested in the successful implementation of assessing student affairs programs, resources, and services can incorporate technology effectively into their day-to-day practice. For example, a director of student activities could use a polling device to collect perceptions about an event or a coordinator of multicultural affairs could effectively integrate technology into marketing for Black History Month.

Intellectual resources. Developing an infrastructure for student affairs assessment allows a division to identify knowledge staff members possess. Such resources are also known as *intellectual capital*, defined as the collective experiences, knowledge, and skills individuals within an organization possess (Klein, 2009). Managing such capital is more than just managing the people who develop processes and procedures; it is the process of documenting how things are done. The danger is that when people leave, they take knowledge with them, resulting in stalled processes or retreating back to old (and outdated) systems. As assessment infrastructure is implemented, it is important to audit what is known and what gaps of knowledge exist. Plans to fill such gaps are vital in making improvements.

Keeping resources in mind matters when implementing infrastructure: Managing resources is an important part of any student affairs work. Therefore, assessment practices and the infrastructure that dictates those practices must be cognizant of the fiscal, human, technological, and intellectual resources within a division of student affairs. Such awareness can help create an assessment infrastructure that attends to the changing environment of student affairs in modern-day higher education.

In this section we have explained that infrastructure brings about intentionality, aids in promoting effectiveness, and supports goals of properly managing resources. Once the case has been made for assessment infrastructure, the next consideration is what to include. Key components are highlighted in the next section.

Sustaining Assessment Practice Through Infrastructure

When considering what is included in student affairs infrastructure, as with any process, context matters: Your institution's resources influence how assessment infrastructure is developed and how efficiently that infrastructure can meet the needs of the diverse functions included within the division. Regardless of context and resources, there are key components of assessment infrastructure. This section addresses three components of assessment infrastructure that are particularly important and how they may be enacted within a division's assessment cycle: (a) divisional mission, goals, and outcomes; (b) divisional and departmental annual planning and assessment processes; and (c) procedures for collecting evidence and reporting results ongoing.

Clarifying Divisional and Departmental Mission, Goals, and Outcomes

It is important to begin each year with an examination of division priorities (Schuh, 2013). Internal and external constituents look to a division of student affairs' mission statement as a demonstration of purpose. Accordingly, a strong mission statement is an important component of good assessment infrastructure. In addition, departmental goals and outcomes should be guided by those of the division. The goals and outcomes at the divisional and departmental levels should inform practice at the program or activity level.

For example, a student affairs *division* identifies "wellness and resilience" as a broad-based learning domain, stating that students will "develop lifelong strategies to optimize health behaviors and establish healthy coping skills." A campus recreation *department* focuses on the specific outcome of "helping students identify tactics to monitor health." A coordinator of health programs within campus recreation develops an activity that has the following learning outcome: "As a result of attending a group exercise class, attendees will be able to correctly measure their resting heart rate." To demonstrate the extent to which the divisional outcome is accomplished at the departmental and activity levels, the health programs coordinator in the department focuses on gathering data on whether participants can correctly take their resting heart rates by observing such behavior and documenting it through a rubric. The findings are then shared with participants as well as with the unit's leadership. Depending on the findings, campus recreation staff members then become empowered to make decisions affecting the program's future.

This example gives insight into how divisional goals are a source of guidance for assessment practices. Using divisional goals, a department can determine actions they will take and what assessment activities they will enact to determine if the goals were met. These processes are essential parts of the assessment cycles we have explained in this chapter. Therefore, having the goals and outcomes clearly stated is pivotal to enacting assessment infrastructure. It can be easy to try to assess too much or too often, particularly when departments have so much "noise" above them between divisional goals and outcomes. Keeping this in mind, another essential part of any assessment infrastructure is to have an annual planning process.

Schedule of Annual Assessment Practices and Planning Processes

Staff members should be clear on the times during the year in which they will be asked to develop action items to help a division of student affairs fulfill its mission and accomplish strategic priorities (Culp & Dungy, 2012). The programs, services, and activities detailed through the assessment cycle should be identified at the start of the academic year. Staff members should never be unsure about when they will be asked to conduct planning processes or the periods in which assessment data collection will be a divisional priority.

At the University of Memphis, planning documents for the next academic year are drafted during December and January of the prior academic year. For example, the 2015–2016 planning document, which goes into effect on July 1, 2015, is drafted by each department head in December 2014. In January 2015, the proposed plan is reviewed by the vice president for student affairs and her associate vice president group. Feedback on the plan is provided by the end of February. Until the end of June, deans and directors are able to revise their 2015–2016 planning document as they also complete their annual reports. Both documents are due by the end of June. Revisions on the planning document coinciding with developing departmental annual reports results in an opportunity to connect reporting and planning in order to use assessment results to inform future goals.

Opportunities for Ongoing Reporting of Results

Collecting data at the program level, consistent with the assessment cycle, encourages staff to analyze and utilize assessment findings to enhance or modify programs, services, and activities in the near term. As explained previously, the University of Memphis uses the end of the spring semester into the beginning of summer (through June) to conduct its reporting process. The reports should connect back to the planning document and highlight all assessment efforts. Evidence from assessment efforts is vital for showcasing the extent to which a task was achieved. Once reports are compiled, an assessment coordinator can develop internal and external annual reports. Holding forums for staff members to share assessment findings with departmental and divisional leaders during this time is a good opportunity to not only identify what has worked well but also give divisional leadership the chance to recognize deans and directors who are contributing to evidence-based practices in student affairs work. It is also recommended that annual reports inform resource allocation and other data-driven decisions (Schuh, 2013).

Furthermore, staff members should seek out opportunities to share feedback from program stakeholders—students, families, faculty, and staff—with program participants and service users following the collection of data (Culp & Dungy, 2012; Schuh, 2013). This is especially important when their feedback enhances the program or service or contributes to decisions associated with the program's future delivery. Advising stakeholders of decisions based on their feedback furthers confidence in the assessment cycle as well as the divisions' and departments' leadership.

This section focused on key components of assessment infrastructure. Divisional mission, goals, and outcomes set the course for departments to follow. Given that assessment must be conducted with intention, a planning process during which action items for the upcoming year are developed should be a key part of assessment infrastructure. Finally, opportunities to report on results and promote findings will help tell the student affairs story and show internal and external stakeholders, how student affairs is contributing to the institution. Now that we have addressed why infrastructure matters and identified some key components of assessment infrastructure, it is important to examine how to keep the infrastructure in place.

Strategies to Sustaining Assessment Infrastructure in Student Affairs

Knowing why assessment infrastructure matters and what should be included is vital to good student affairs assessment practice. However, understanding and doing are different from creating long-standing functional systems that are efficient and effective. For assessment coordinators to see these practices become a part of the culture of a division of student affairs, they must enact certain approaches and practices within the infrastructure. Two strategies are recommended to keep assessment in the forefront of staff members' minds, particularly early on as coordinators develop assessment infrastructure: Aid staff in increasing assessment competence and confidence and recognize the impact of good assessment.

Support Competence and Confidence

Many staff members do not believe they have "research skills," which can undermine the assessment culture. They believe they need to "do data collection" and may not feel prepared to complete the collection, analysis, and interpretation of data (Bresciani, 2010; Green, Jones, & Aloi, 2008). Assessment seems scary because staff members feel underprepared to conduct this part of their work. While assessment coordinators should help staff understand the distinction between research and assessment, there still is a common goal of collecting evidence that can be used and done in a way that has a good methodological approach. These practices are not of interest to some student affairs professionals, and they may fear that their skills are deficient, which might result in them doing something wrong and damaging the credibility of their activity, program, or department.

Student affairs staff members typically do not enter the field with strong assessment and research backgrounds (Dickerson et al., 2011). Therefore, an assessment coordinator must work collaboratively with staff within the units to develop the skills to conduct acceptable assessment practices as a part of modern-day student affairs practice. For example, staff members need to conceive of assessment as an approach to their work rather than as an add-on to their work. As a result of this paradigm shift, staff members can integrate the assessment cycle—sometimes unconsciously—into efforts to develop and enact programs or provide services.

The importance of investing in staff members' continuing education, particularly in the area of assessment, cannot be emphasized enough. Developing programs and workshops such as those at the University of Memphis can help staff members identify key competencies on which to improve, including assessment. For example, each March the division of student affairs has a spring break professional development challenge. During this time, staff members are challenged to participate in as many workshops as possible. Typically 10 workshops are hosted, each one focused on a specific student affairs professional competency identified by ACPA and NASPA (American College Personnel Association & National Association of Student Personnel Administrators, 2010). Assessment, evaluation, and research (AER) form a competency always popular with staff members because they know the vice president for student affairs is particularly interested in evidence-based practices. In addition to the spring break challenge, the division hosts an assessment boot camp each summer. Student affairs leadership at the University of Memphis uses "downtimes" each year, such as spring break and summertime, to provide professional development sessions for staff. Hosting workshops on assessment has been a priority within the division for almost 10 years. Mitigating residual "fears" associated with "doing assessment" will go a long way in refining goals, developing high-quality assessments, and delivering the best possible programs to stakeholders.

Recognizing the Impact of Good Assessment

Another key element of assessment infrastructure is creating the systems to recognize good assessment work. Often, it is this recognition that promotes buy-in for the process and its results. Taking time to reflect on the assessment process and findings allows staff members to make the connection that what they do contributes to more than just the success of their individual programs. Reflecting on how well they did with such processes, staff members focus on what can be done better and celebrate the accomplishments of the department and division. As assessment coordinators create ways to recognize the impact of good assessment they might consider the following:

- What incentives encourage staff members to integrate assessment into their work?
- What tangible and intrinsic rewards are provided for staff members who contribute to the fulfillment of the division's and department's goals and outcomes?
- What needs to happen for staff members to continue to focus on good assessment work and/or develop strategies to improve their assessment practices?

A reward is recognition for some level of competence, and staff members may find that a reward prompts them to identify new goals to improve how they conduct assessment. Tangible benefits, such as awards programs, positive performance evaluations, or being asked to share findings to colleagues, more explicitly honor staff members who buy in to the assessment infrastructure.

While rewards will help, there may also be a need to implement systems that address poor assessment practice. For example, tying the allocation of financial and human resources may be leveraged as a "stick" for programs or departments that do not integrate an assessment infrastructure consistent with divisional expectations. Some assessment coordinators might work with their divisional leaders to develop an approach to helping staff with improvement plans. These plans outline steps for improvement and implications if staff members do not commit to changes. Ultimately, coordinators should help diminish fear and support increased competence; however, for staff members that avoid doing assessment out of fear or a perceived lack of competence, systems of accountability should be enacted.

Conclusion: Even With a Map, You Still Need a Plan

We have relied on the opening highway analogy to emphasize the importance of infrastructure in realizing good assessment practices in student affairs. The NHS is well documented on maps—paper and virtual—that depict its vast existence. Millions upon millions of travelers drive the highway system every year. And yet, even with a vast infrastructure like the NHS, travelers still require a plan. Assessment in student affairs work also requires a plan.

The use of an assessment cycle provides a proposed framework for divisions, departments, and staff to use when developing, delivering, and assessing programs, services, and activities. The assessment cycle provides a framework to establish infrastructure. But every campus experience is slightly different based on resources or other contributing factors, to their assessment journey.

Much like an overhaul of the NHS, integrating the assessment cycle into a division's work must occur piece-by-piece. Beginning a construction project on the NHS all at once would do one thing— shut down the entire highway system. Similarly, a division cannot enact assessment infrastructure overnight. After an audit of what attributes of infrastructure are in place, the case can be made for why the infrastructure must be strengthened and what components need to be added. Developing divisional goals and outcomes, planning for the implementation, and conducting annual reporting to collect and share evidence are vital processes. Finally, systems must be in place to sustain assessment infrastructure. Connecting all that staff members do back to divisional priorities can help assessment coordinators make the case that assessment of programs, resources, and services can be a professionally rewarding experience and an opportunity for staff members to demonstrate exceptional confidence in their student affairs practice.

References

American College Personnel Association & National Association of Student Personnel Administrators. (2010). *ACPA/NASPA professional competency areas for student affairs practitioners*. Retrieved from www.myacpa.org/professional-com petency-areas-student-affairs-practitioners

Bresciani, M. (2010). Assessment and evaluation. In J. H. Schuh, S. R. Jones, S. R. Harper (Eds.), *Student services: A handbook for the profession* (pp. 321–334). San Francisco, CA: Jossey-Bass.

Collins, K. M., & Roberts, D. M. (Eds.). (2012). *Learning is not a sprint: Assessing and documenting student leader learning in cocurricular involvement.* Washington, DC: NASPA Student Affairs Administrators in Higher Education.

Culp, M. M., & Dungy, G. J. (Eds.). (2012). *Building a culture of evidence in student affairs: A guide for leaders and practitioners.* Washington, DC: NASPA Student Affairs Administrators in Higher Education.

Dalton, J. C. (2003). Managing human resources. In S. R. Komives & D. B. Woodard Jr. (Eds.), *Student services: A handbook for the profession* (pp. 397–420). San Francisco, CA: Jossey-Bass.

Dickerson, A. M., Hoffman, J. L., Anan, B. P., Brown, K. F., Vong, L. K., & Bresciani, M. (2011). A comparison of senior student affairs officer and student affairs preparatory program faculty expectations of entry-level professionals' competencies. *Journal of Student Affairs Research and Practice, 48*(4), 463–479.

Green, A. S., Jones, E., & Aloi, S. (2008). An exploration of high-quality student affairs learning outcomes assessment practices. *NASPA Journal, 45*(1), 133–157.

Junco, R. (2014). *Engaging students through social media: Evidence-based practices for use in student affairs.* San Francisco, CA: Jossey-Bass.

Klein, D. A. (1998). *The strategic management of intellectual capital.* Boston, MA: Butterworth-Heinemann.

Maki, P. M. (2004). *Assessing for learning: Building a sustainable commitment across the institution.* Sterling, VA: Stylus.

Schuh, J. H. (2003). Strategic planning and finance. In S. R. Komives & D. B. Woodard Jr. (Eds.), *Student services: A handbook for the profession* (pp. 358–378). San Francisco, CA: Jossey-Bass.

Schuh, J. H. (2013). Developing a culture of assessment in student affairs. *New Directions for Student Services, 142,* 89–105.

Schuh, J., & Gansemer-Topf, A. (2010). *The role of student affairs in student learning assessment.* Urbana: University of Illinois and Indiana University, National Institute for Learning Outcomes Assessment. Retrieved from www.learningoutcomeassessment.org/documents/studentAffairsrole.pdf

Suskie, L. (2009). *Assessing student learning: A common sense guide.* San Francisco, CA: Wiley and Sons.

Yousey, K. M. (2006). The best of both worlds: Coupling research and assessment. *About Campus, 2*(4), 23–25.

Yousey, K. M., Elkins, B., & Timm, D. (2007). *Proceedings from ACPA 2007: The student affairs assessment conference.* Columbus, OH.

Yousey-Elsener, K. M. (2013). *Successful assessment in student affairs: A how-to guide.* Little Falls, NJ: PaperClip Communications.

4 Tenet Four: Leading Logistical and Administrative Assessment Tasks in Student Affairs

Justin Keen

THIS CHAPTER focuses on the logistical aspects of student affairs assessment practice. It defines *logistics* broadly as the interrelated set of structures, relationships, and operational procedures that necessarily underlie assessment practice, including organizational structure, strategic resource planning, and project planning. In particular, it explores the logistics of student affairs assessment through three connected organizing considerations:

1. **Organizational Structure.** Where do/should assessment professionals exist in relationship to the overall structure of student affairs organizations, and what implication does this placement have for coordinating assessment activities?
2. **Strategic Resource Planning and Allocation.** What processes exist for long-term financial and human resource planning with the goal of assessment capacity development, and how can these long-term plans be best actualized in annual budgets and other short-term plans?
3. **Project Planning.** What techniques can be used to support the logistic coordination and successful completion of individual assessment projects?

Based on these questions, this chapter starts with the assumption that one size will not fit all when it comes to coordinating excellent student affairs assessment practice. For readers interested in common practices related to these questions, the Student Affairs

Assessment Leaders (SAAL) organization has additional, and likely more pragmatic, resources related to these questions.

Organizational Structure

The relationship of assessment positions to the overall organizational structure of student affairs units has important implications for how assessment practices are coordinated. Bresciani (2012) stated that the responsibilities of research and assessment in student affairs belonged to every member of the profession. Because it is a shared responsibility, assessment practice should cut across the traditional, hierarchical structures that dominate organizational design in student affairs (Kuk, 2012). In a hierarchical organization, the unit's mission is divided into a set of self-sufficient departments that fulfill their aspects of the mission largely independently through top-down management structures. This hierarchical structure creates significant challenges for assessment, a process that often requires professionals to collaborate outside this structure and be empowered to make changes based on results.

Kuk (2012) noted that while most traditional student affairs practices are linked vertically with individuals interacting through a chain of command (an assistant director reports to an associate director who reports to a director), assessment practitioners are part of a new set of specialists (including communications professionals and others) who primarily connect horizontally to a variety of staff members across the student affairs enterprise. Through these horizontal connections, the assessment specialists in the student affairs organizational structure can be better viewed as members of many cross-functional teams rather than as equal but separate partners in a siloed environment (or as special advisers to a vice president fulfilling a top-down leadership role). In other words, it is more important that assessment professionals are developing connections to staff across the division than where they report in the organizational chart. The work of assessment is a shared responsibility rather than something that can be siloed in one part of the organization.

This horizontal structure encourages collective problem solving (invaluable in closing the loop on the assessment cycle). However, problems can arise as the two different ways of assigning and accomplishing work (horizontal and vertical) coexist in the same organization (Kuk, 2012). This is particularly true for logistics, where tasks that would be relatively simple in a vertical structure, such as determining what unit should fund what practice, are much more open to interpretation in horizontal structures. Although assessment could exist in a purely vertical structure, where all assessment is conceived of and completed by a specialized assessment unit acting as an external evaluator, this siloed vision is antithetical to the capacity-building approach espoused by this volume.

Yet, assessment specialists must work in a historically vertical organizational structure; placement within that structure can open and close doors. Responsibility for developing assessment capacity can be placed in a variety of organizational roles, including, but not limited to, offices with multiple professionals reporting to a vice president or assistant vice president, an assistant vice president who has assessment as part of his or her portfolio, solitary directors reporting to vice presidents or assistant vice presidents, solitary coordinators reporting at any level of the organization, and staff members with other responsibilities who take on assessment as an additional charge. Attention to institutional culture is a vital consideration in deciding where assessment specialists should reside within an organizational structure. In some cultures, being as close to the top of the organization as possible may communicate that assessment is valued. This proximity to leadership also helps assessment specialists advocate to leadership for strong and persistent messages about assessment and related strategic processes. In other cultures, placement in a particular wing of an organization, such as in the dean of students' team, may open up unique collaborative opportunities.

The physical location of an office flows from this set of decisions. Regular informal access to divisional leaders may be an important consideration. Ease of access to and proximity of other staff may be equally important. Some assessment specialists make a point of always traveling to meetings in their collaborators' offices, which increases visibility and reduces the drawbacks of any particular office location.

The sociogram, a technique commonly used by resident assistants in residence halls (Ball State University, 2012; Lake Erie College, 2011), can be a useful tool for mapping the ways in which an assessment position shares authority and responsibility as a member of a variety of teams. A *sociogram* is a graphical representation of the connections between individuals. Completing a sociogram that depicts these interrelationships may be a useful first step in understanding how an assessment role or department relates or should relate to other areas or individuals in a student affairs organization. It may also be useful in exposing a set of more detailed logistical questions, such as the following: What communication pathways need to be opened to accomplish assessment goals? What areas of the organization need to develop new assessment leaders? How is funding or staffing a particular assessment project accomplished? How does an assessment professional respond to conflicting requests (or time demands) from two different areas of the organization?

Strategic Resource Planning and Allocation

Schuh et al. (2001) identified lack of money and lack of expertise as two important barriers to quality assessment practice in student affairs. These two barriers are interrelated in that the majority of resources expended in many assessment activities are in the form of staff time. Any logistical system that supports both the continual development of assessment capacity and the fulfillment of that capacity in quality assessment work must have a solid financial and human foundation on which to operate. A long-term strategic plan for developing assessment capacity within a division is vital to ensuring that limited resources are available where they are most important.

The Council for the Advancement of Standards in Higher Education (CAS) (2012) suggests that assessment offices must have the financial resources to support "study conceptualization, data collection, data entry and analysis, dissemination of assessment and research findings, and methodological training of staff" (pp. 34–35). This set of activities also highlights the complexity of looking at all financial resources supporting assessment projects as a single budget. Likely, funds and staff time from throughout the student affairs unit will support various assessment projects. The metaphor of assessment specialist as capacity builder is instructive here. Resources related to completing individual assessment projects are likely to be spread across the division. However, resources related to assessment capacity development could be centralized into a single assessment budget. Consequently, this section focuses on methods for directing money and time to developing divisional assessment capacity rather than supporting individual assessment projects.

Resources supporting assessment specialists and the development of assessment capacity are often centralized into a single budget. Some common budget items include the following:

- Assessment staffing, including professionals, graduate assistants, and student workers
- Basic office expenses, including hardware and supplies to support assessment staff productivity
- Educational and knowledge resources, such as books on assessment, webinars, and copies of seminal professional publications and standards
- Money to support staff attendance at national and regional assessment conferences
- Fees and incentives for benchmarking surveys such as the NASPA research consortium surveys and the National Survey of Student Engagement or topical instruments developed by the Education Advisory Board, Noel-Levitz, and other organizations
- Assessment support services such as Campus Labs, Qualtrics, and SurveyMonkey that provide tools to create, distribute, and analyze surveys and, in some cases, provide more comprehensive assessment consulting services and resource banks
- Software for data analysis and presentation such as IBM SPSS (for statistical analysis), NVivo (for qualitative research), and Tableau (for data visualization)
- Printing and other costs associated with conducting communication plans and transparency strategies
- Hardware, such as card readers to support participant tracking and tablets for live survey data collection

If some or all of these resources are included in a centralized budget, it makes sense to develop a long-term financial plan for assessment spending to help direct decisions about how money dedicated for developing assessment capacity can best be spent. Conneely (2010) described strategic planning as integral to financial planning in student affairs because it creates a context for making financial decisions in pursuit of long-term goals. Decisions related to both financial planning and time usage can be made more intentionally if they occur in the context of a wider strategic plan for assessment. Conneely (2010) outlined one process that could be used to develop and sustain a multiyear assessment strategic plan. The process includes the following:

1. Identify the needs and priorities of the plan.
2. Understand the factors and assumptions used to build the financial model.
3. Determine the time span of the plan.
4. Implement the plan.
5. Conduct assessment to measure the success of the plan (p. 55).

The first three steps in this process can be used to form a strategic plan that identifies long-term priorities. The final two steps involve making adjustments to activities as time passes and allowing the plan to evolve to meet changing circumstances.

Bers and Mittler (1996) described the use of an assessment audit that could be an instructive starting point for identifying needs and priorities. On one campus, the researchers interviewed all administrators, faculty, and staff who had a role in assessment, from frontline practitioners to high-level administrators. The audit revealed crucial information about cultural practices related to assessment, including the abundance of information, relative paucity of data use or intentionality behind collection, fear of the burden of assessment practices, participants who were doing assessment activities but did not define them as such, mixed reactions as to the value of assessment, and limits of the information system for analysis and collaboration. These findings represent both potential barriers and assets to the capacity-building process. If this audit is replicated in student affairs, it is important to consider which stakeholders should be included. In particular, partners of student affairs across the university, including faculty and students, are important stakeholders in student affairs assessment practice and probably warrant inclusion in such an audit.

Alternative approaches to the audit practice are numerous. Some units use an internal review process, such as the one provided by

CAS (2012). Others use alternative frameworks (this book could serve as one) or hire external consultants who bring their own frameworks to the investigation and analysis. No matter what technique is used, the process of identifying the gaps between the current state of divisional assessment capacity and the desired future state forms the basis for a strategic plan that can inform decision making and prioritization.

The findings of an assessment audit or another form of environmental scan are often depicted in a gap analysis that involves comparing the current environment for assessment with the desired future environment (envisioned wonderfully by this book's other chapters). Decisions regarding how financial resources and staff time are applied to close these gaps can then be adjusted on a regular basis to ensure continual improvement in closing gaps.

Cyclic Budgeting in Student Affairs Practice

Taking an assessment strategic plan as its foundation, the practical aspects of budget and time management on a year-to-year basis are likely to be constrained by institutional context, policy, procedures, and preferred standards of behavior. Although these factors may constrain access to resources for assessment, they are unlikely to completely discourage strategic allocation of assessment resources. Barr and McClellan (2011) provided an overview of the most common budgeting models in higher education, some of which are explained in subsequent sections. These can be instructive, both in understanding institutional and divisional budgeting processes and in making intentional choices about how to adjust resource use to meet long-term goals on a yearly basis. According to Barr and McClellan (2011), most institutions use a hybrid of these approaches. Types of institutional budgeting, such as formula budgeting, are left off this list because, although they form an important surround for budgeting for assessment work, they are not particularly useful for thinking about the management of yearly assessment budgets.

- **Incremental-based budgeting.** All areas receive equal percentage increases/decreases. This is a common form and is most used in stable environments that lack emerging needs.

- **Initiative-based budgeting.** All areas return a portion of the budgets yearly (presumably from cut programs or other savings) to a collective pot and then can apply to receive money from that pot for new programs.
- **Performance-based budgeting.** Future resources are distributed based on the success of past programs measured by prespecified performance metrics.
- **Zero-based budgeting.** Budgets are redeveloped from scratch, usually on a yearly basis, and each initiative that could be funded is rejustified or cut. In this method, potential new initiatives are considered equal to existent initiatives. This process is challenging and time-consuming to enact in large organizations and may be more appropriate for small budgets or operations.

Aspects of each of these models can be implemented as part of a yearly budgeting process for assessment, even if the prevalent budget model in a campus is at odds with that model. For instance, even if a student affairs unit using incremental budgeting increases or decreases an assessment budget by 5% in a given year, that does not mean that all line items in the assessment budget must be increased or decreased by a corresponding amount. Rather, an assessment team could enact a hybrid of the initiative-based and performance-based models in an attempt to cut tactics that had not been working as planned and replace them with new items they hope will help the team pursue its strategic agenda with renewed vigor.

These budgeting models can be useful for strategically aligning time to assessment priorities. Budgeting time is just as important, if not more important, than money. More often than not in student affairs, we are our most expensive (and valuable) resources. From a strategic perspective, it will be useful to do the two activities together; doing so may illuminate some valuable opportunities for trade-offs between the two.

Project Planning

Coordinating large assessment projects can feel a bit like herding cats. Projects that require many staff members to buy in to a single process and work together in different roles can feature communication gaps or crossed priorities that spiral into insurmountable barriers. Furthermore, in most circumstances no one staff member involved in a project will have the necessary skill, time, and positional power to lead all aspects of the process.

Bresciani, Gardner, and Hickmott (2009) suggest the following set of questions that could be asked to determine the costs (both financial and temporal) of individual assessment projects:

- What types of instruments or methodologies will be used to collect the data?
- How will the data be analyzed and by whom?
- What types of technology and technological support will be used?
- Who will be involved in the assessment process, and in what ways?
- How will the results of the assessment be communicated?
- What kinds of professional development are needed to implement the planned assessment methods, data analysis, interpretation of the data, and communication of the findings? (p. 160)

Answering these questions could provide a useful road map for what goes into an assessment project, though it is unlikely to yield a particularly systematic approach. Workflow management could be a useful guide for a systematic approach for managing the logistics of individual assessment projects.

Workflow management has become an increasingly popular solution to the mirror of these problems in information technology. Workflow diagrams depict the business activities related to an overall process in such a way that activities can be performed consistently and reliably. General workflow processes can be designed and tailored to individual projects, so that a single general process could support multiple assessment projects with divergent methods (Mangan & Sadiq, 2002). Looking at an assessment project as a workflow collaborated on by multiple individuals has the advantage of providing an opportunity to have those individuals make commitments to completing various parts of the process.

The assessment cycle (Bresciani, 2003) serves as an ideal workflow process for individual assessment projects. Depicted as a workflow (see Figure 4.1), assessment projects proceed through four steps: establish goals, match with opportunities, gather data, and use results.

Figure 4.1   The assessment cycle workflow.

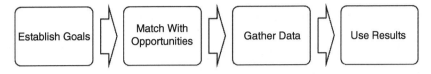

These steps can be complicated logistically, as each may involve multiple staff members and require access to particular resources and expertise. Using this four-step process as a general guide, assessment projects can be mapped out in advance of the project. To create a workflow plan, staff identify who would be involved in and responsible for each aspect of the process. Additional resources can be aligned to steps in the process where they are necessary.

Visualizing the assessment cycle workflow can help staff members understand and commit to their roles in the process. This can be particularly important for the redesign or improvement phase, also termed *closing the loop*. Many wonderful assessment projects have failed to leave a lasting impact because no human resources were assigned to close the loop.

This four-step workflow may underestimate the number of unique tasks that actually go into completing an assessment project. Schuh et al. (2001) presented an 11-step process that could be used as an alternative workflow map, but it lacks the same concentration on closing the assessment loop. For a particularly complicated assessment project, this process could be a useful alternative particularly if adapted to include a final step of closing the loop. Ultimately, the complexity of how the workflow is tracked should be based on what is most useful for keeping the team on the same page and ensuring that the process keeps moving.

Once the process is under way, tracking the project through a graphical representation known as a burn-down chart (Figure 4.2) can be helpful in depicting where the project is in its life cycle and identifying barriers to the project's success that may have surfaced. A burn-down chart depicts estimated remaining time to project completion on the x-axis and the workflow on the y-axis. A line is then drawn to represent the ideal timeline for completing the workflow steps. A second line is drawn as the project is being completed that

Figure 4.2   Assessment cycle burn-down chart example.

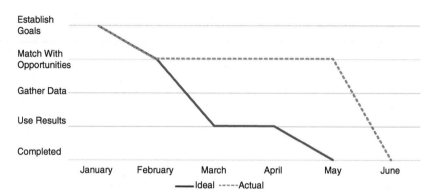

depicts how the actual process played out. These charts provide a clear picture of where and how a project hit logistical barriers. It can also provide a potential measure for efficiency of the assessment process (Kocurek, 2011). Figure 4.2 depicts a burn-down chart for a project that fell behind after the assessment was not administered when originally intended. Staff made a clear push in June to finish the project one month late.

Banta and Blaich (2010) discussed the challenge that higher education has experienced with closing the loop and completing the assessment process by making changes based on results. Viewing the assessment cycle as a workflow and using burn-down charts can help highlight this challenge by identifying projects that went dormant before the loop was closed. In particular, Banta and Blaich (2010) highlighted the importance of connecting stakeholders to the decision-making process in a meaningful and intentional way. This aspect of the assessment workflow is likely to rely on and tax the horizontal relationships of assessment practitioners more than other aspects of the process.

Conclusion

Logistics and the set of techniques by which resources are aligned to assessment needs are important considerations in developing and realizing assessment capacity. This chapter provides a variety of techniques that could be useful in developing approaches to logistical assessment challenges, including budgeting and time management, project management, and dynamics of organizational design, and many more tools exist in the repertoires of student affairs assessment professionals. A single theme that binds these tools together is that they are best engaged in collaboratively. Student affairs professionals are not soldiers in an assessment army. Rather they are important decision makers in and leaders of assessment processes. By bringing this set of tools to their collaborations, student affairs assessment professionals can help teams build logistical systems that realize assessment capacity.

The following questions summarize this chapter and may be helpful in setting up the logistics aspects of an assessment office or role:

- Who should be tasked with building assessment capacity? Who should they report to? Where should their offices be located? With whom do they need to develop robust collaborations?
- What is the (strategic) plan for developing assessment capacity? How can this plan be used to inform allocation of resources to assessment priorities? What assessment-related resources should be funded by a dedicated assessment budget?
- What project-planning methods should be employed as guidelines in developing and completing assessment projects? What methods support consistency in closing the loop on assessment projects?

References

Ball State University. (2012). *Resident assistant manual 2012–2013*. Muncie, OH: Ball State University.

Banta, T. W., & Blaich, C. (2010). Closing the assessment loop. *Change: The Magazine of Higher Learning, 43*(1), 22–27.

Barr, M. J., & McClellen, G. S. (2011). *Budgets and financial management in higher education*. San Francisco, CA: Jossey-Bass.

Bers, T., & Mittler, M. L. (1996). Taking the first step: An assessment audit. In T. W. Banta, J. P. Lind, K. E. Black, & F. W. Oblander (Eds.), *Assessment in practice: Putting principles to work on college campuses* (pp. 322–325). San Francisco, CA: Jossey-Bass.

Bresciani, M. J. (2003). Expert driven assessment: Making it meaningful to decision makers. *ECAR Research Bulletin, 21*.

Bresciani, M. J. (2012). Changing roles and responsibilities in student affairs research and assessment. In A. Tull & L. Kuk (Eds.), *New realities in the management of student affairs: Emerging specialist roles and structures for changing times* (pp. 107–114). Sterling, VA: Stylus.

Bresciani, M. J., Gardner, M. M., & Hickmott, J. (2009). *Demonstrating student success: A practical guide to outcomes-based assessment of learning and development in student affairs.* Sterling, VA: Stylus.

Conneely, J. F. (2010). Strategic planning and financial management. *New Directions for Student Services, 132,* 51–61.

Council for the Advancement of Standards in Higher Education. (2012). *CAS self-assessment guide for assessment services.* Washington, DC: Council for the Advancement of Standards in Higher Education.

Kocurek, D. (2011). Understanding the scrum burndown chart. *Methods and Tools.* Retrieved from www.methodsandtools.com/archive/scrumburndown.php

Kuk, L. (2012). The context for using specialist roles and matric structures in student affairs organizations. In A. Tull & L. Kuk (Eds.), *New realities in the management of student affairs: Emerging specialist roles and structures for changing times* (pp. 21–38). Sterling, VA: Stylus.

Lake Erie College. (2011). *Resident assistant manual 2011–2012.* Painesville, OH: Lake Erie College.

Mangan, P., & Sadiq, S. (2002). On building workflow models for flexible processes. *Australian Computer Science Communications, 23*(2), 103–109.

Schuh, J. H., Upcraft, M. L., & Associates. (2001). *Assessment practice in student affairs: An application manual.* San Francisco, CA: Jossey-Bass.

5 Tenet Five: Using Technology to Advance Assessment

Erin M. Bentrim
Ted Elling

THE AMERICAN Association for Higher Education (AAHE) first published "Seven Principles for Good Practice in Undergraduate Education" in 1987 (Chickering & Gamson, 1987). Since that time, hundreds of thousands of copies have been distributed across the United States and Canada. In 1996, Chickering and Ehrmann wrote a complementary piece titled "Implementing the Seven Principles: Technology as a Lever." The impact of both of these publications has been far-reaching and continues to be applicable in institutions of higher education today. Evidence of this appears in the 2010 National Education Technology Plan from the U.S. Department of Education, titled *Transforming American Education: Learning Powered by Technology*. The overall focus of the plan calls for "applying the advanced technologies used in our daily personal and professional lives to our entire education system to improve student learning, accelerate and scale up the adoption of effective practices, and use data and information for continuous improvement" (p. iv).

One primary goal of that plan addresses assessment and measuring what matters by using technology as the lever. The report argues that the power of technology is not being used to its full capability when it comes to assessment and stresses the need for data-driven decision making that positively affects all students. The primary rationale behind assessment is to ensure continual improvement of programs and services for students, as well as promote accountability for student learning. The challenge is making the "relevant data available to the right people at the right time, and in the right form" (Chickering & Ehrmann, 1996, pp. 3–4.)

There is no shortage of data in institutions of higher education. As student populations become more diverse, budgets become more constrained, and learning environments become more complex, adopting and integrating technology as a means for assessment in student affairs is vital. "We are now entering an era in which learning may occur anywhere, at any time, with multiple devices" (Macfayden, Dawson, Pardo, & Gasevic, 2014, p. 22).

Bentrim and Henning refer to the role of the assessment coordinator as technology administrator in Chapter 1. This might come in the form of managing, recommending, or developing systems while simultaneously acting as support staff. The assessment coordinator is often responsible for managing the data-tracking technology used in the division while also using technology to retrieve data quickly and efficiently.

As capacity builders, assessment coordinators use technology as a tool to implement organizational change and improvement within the division. Doing so allows for successful fulfillment of the mission and vision of the institution. In fact, while investigating the strategies of highly productive and successful institutions of higher education, Auguste, Cota, Jayaram, and Laboissiere (2010) found leadership and technology infrastructures to be two of the five factors of organizational capacity that successful and productive institutions possess. Documenting college impact on student success is a complex process, and determining which tools are appropriately suited for the task can be daunting. Yet choosing the optimal one is essential to the success of an assessment program. This chapter provides overarching guidance regarding what questions to ask when making a decision on how to choose technology tools.

Integrating Technology Into Data Collection

It is important to remember in all of this planning that technology is not something that happens to us. It is something we create. We must not confuse a tool with a goal. We must, therefore, be sure that technology serves the fundamental purposes of higher education. That will be more difficult than it sounds. (Katz, 2001, para. 28)

The history of technology playing a role in higher education and measuring the impact it can have on the lives of students and the work of administrators dates back to some of the earliest student affairs conference proceedings, according to archives documenting the history of higher education. For example, a new audio-recording concept was introduced at the 1950 National Association of Student Personnel Administrators Conference. The idea was to have those who were experienced in the field have their professional advice and experiences recorded so others could listen and learn at their own convenience. At this same conference, a vendor demonstrated the innovative use of the new Polaroid camera to create student identification cards (Guidry, 2012).

Another example of administrative functionality in higher education systems changing based on technology shifts can be found in the process of course registration as it transitioned from physical sign-ups in large gymnasiums utilizing index cards to track classroom seats (1960s), to punch cards to enter that data into a student information system (1970s), to phone-based registration (1980s), and finally to online registration (1990s), allowing students to register for classes anywhere they could obtain an Internet connection (Elling & Brown, 2001).

Data gathering and data analysis have followed similar advancement trajectories as technology morphed from hand-tabulated paper surveys; to bubble-sheet-based paper surveys that could be scanned for analysis; to online surveys, e-mail or hyperlink-accessible, that could be instantly tabulated and reported from an assessment software system.

Advances in data-gathering technology have greatly influenced the way in which assessment coordinators operate and manage data at unit and division levels. The implications of this reality are that coordinators must be not only competent and skilled in assessment but also proficient at addressing issues related to technology. At the very least, nurturing partnerships with others on campus who can serve as resources is necessary. In order to be successful, assessment coordinators must be open to change and serve as a catalyst for moving others forward in technological advances. Often, staff members are already fearful of assessment, and introducing technology into the mix requires another layer of facilitation and role-modeling behaviors on the part of assessment coordinators to reduce anxiety.

There are a multitude of tools that integrate technology into data collection, and the tools described in this section are in no way an exhaustive list. Rather, this is a snapshot of those currently in the forefront for discussion purposes. In addition, it is not the editors' intention for this chapter to serve as an endorsement of any tool or system over another. Due diligence is encouraged prior to selecting any tool or system.

Data can come from many sources. Interviews, focus groups, surveys, and document reviews are but a few. The tools used vary according to the needs and scope of a project, but it is likely that for every data source, there is a new way of gathering the information. To put these advances in context, Dillman (1978) advocated a process he labeled the total design method for survey administration. This process involved four mailings, a reminder postcard, personalized and hand-signed cover letters, and the delivery of a second survey by certified mail if a respondent lost the first one. As recently as 20 years ago, this debate over the proper design and administration of mail surveys was still occurring. Obviously, there have been rapid shifts in technologic advances.

Online or Web-Based Survey Technology

On many campuses, surveys are still being administered by pencil and paper. This can be a good way to gather needed information from a captive audience, such as entering students during new student orientation. However, many commercial test vendors are beginning to move toward online or web-based options. One challenge for campuses that prefer administering surveys to large groups of students at once is the logistical issue of finding computer lab space as well as proctors for each area.

Many colleges and universities have access to web-based products such as SurveyMonkey or Qualtrics. While these are simple, quick, and cost-effective ways of gathering data, security breaches and quality control issues must be considered. Many staff members do not have the expertise to craft and design valid and reliable surveys. Another drawback is that the ease of use of these tools lends itself to relying on surveys as the primary method of gathering data, which results in survey fatigue for respondents and can therefore impact response rates.

Clicker Response Systems

A clicker response system may be used in classrooms, during presentations, or at the end of programs to gather information on whatever the facilitator desires. The system consists of both hardware (usually a handheld clicker device and/or app for smartphones and tablets) and software and allows real-time interaction and data collection. For example, a staff member presenting on signs of alcohol poisoning can ask participants what the symptoms are and get immediate feedback on learning. The student "clicks" on what they believe to be the correct answer, and software on the computer collects responses and generates a chart to show how many students responded correctly or incorrectly. This allows the presenter to clarify any misconceptions. Clickers can be used to answer satisfaction questions, take attendance at an event, gather demographic data, and even document peer or group interactions. There are many benefits to gathering data this way, but there can also be some disadvantages. First, the initial system setup can be cost-prohibitive. Second, the logistics of getting the system set up, clickers distributed, and so on, can take up valuable time. Third, using an immediate feedback system like this often requires a presenter to change course at a moment's notice if students are confused.

Card Swipe Technology

Another popular method to gather data is through card swipe technology. Students can swipe their university identification card for entry into events. The data can then be loaded into a spreadsheet, and information can be gathered about those who attended or did not attend. The data can also be linked to other institutional data about the student; therefore, this technology is useful for not only tracking attendance numbers but also providing rich data about student engagement. Research has established that one of the conditions for student success is whether or not a student is involved academically and socially. By tracking student attendance, demographics, retention risk factors, and other student-related variables staff members can target particular students who may need additional support. In addition, using card swipe technology provides evidence of who is *not* attending programs. This information can support decisions on how programming dollars are spent.

This technology is relatively inexpensive and is quite user-friendly. Drawbacks include determining who "owns" the data from the machines. Security issues need to be considered. Another consideration is the unease that students may feel at having their attendance tracked at programs or events of a sensitive nature (e.g., educational events sponsored by the student health center). Discretion should always be used when swiping identification cards and/or sharing the data that are collected.

Mobile Data Gathering

Mobile data gathering is a way to collect data from respondents in real time or near real time. Examples of this mode of data collection include surveys administered on portable devices that can be synced to a network where the data automatically populate an online survey; students using their smartphones or tablets to capture a quick response (QR) code that automatically opens a survey for them to take; e-mail invitations sent to students containing a hyperlink to an online survey (perhaps the most common at this time); and mobile applications that, once downloaded and registered to a mobile device, allow a student to respond to a presentation in the classroom, such as a poll, or to provide immediate feedback to the instructor on the level of knowledge acquisition. Many of these examples are designed to work across multiple platforms and mobile devices, require little or no financial investment on the part of the student, and can be used remotely. Campuses with large populations of distance learners may find these types of data gathering especially powerful.

There are a number of concerns over these types of data collection mechanisms, such as equity and access issues, data security, training staff and students in the use of these systems, and campus-based conversations about standardization of these new methods across the campus. Just as there are multiple clicker vendors, there are multiple applications to consider in any acquisition. A final practical consideration is an assessment of the degree to which the university, its faculty, its staff, and its students are willing to embrace these technologies.

Data Extraction Tools

Another mechanism for gathering data is investigating information already available in existing data sources on campus. Although estimates vary from institution to institution, Nichols (1995) estimated that between 30% and 35% of assessment data might already be available on campus from other assessment activities. This suggests that an inventory of existing data sources should be considered prior to developing additional survey instrumentation. Existing data may take the form of survey responses, biographical and demographic data from student information systems, data repositories, and other departmental data silos. Saunders and Wohlgemuth (2009) emphasize the need to "[use] existing information to support assessment efforts" (p. 47). They also direct student affairs professionals to coordinate and maximize the use of institution-specific information and to share their results with others across the institution.

Perhaps the easiest way to obtain existing data is to work with the owner of the data set. Be prepared to provide specific, detailed information in regard to the data elements desired; the intended use of the data; and the format in which they are needed. Utilizing this method minimizes the need for data extraction tools that often require additional training and cost to the end user. On some campuses, fulfilling this type of data request may require approval of senior leaders. Be sure to explore the process for requesting the data early in the project.

Another approach would be for the assessment coordinator to personally extract the data. There are a number of different data extraction tools on the market. Some of them are self-contained tools within student information systems, stored procedures within a data repository, or a specific stand-alone application on the desktop. Examples of stand-alone applications are standard query language (SQL), WebFocus, BrioQuery, database applications, and some spreadsheets. Each of these tools allows the assessment coordinator to connect electronically to the desired data source, extract a copy of the needed data from the system, and place it into a workspace for further manipulation and analysis.

The examples listed in the previous paragraph are sophisticated data extraction tools that require some familiarity with either a programming language or software-specific coding language in order to extract and use the requested data. Database applications such as Microsoft Access can be configured to link to a desired data source, ask for the desired information (often called a query), and download that information into a local workspace. Benefits of using a database program as a data extraction tool are that a database also allows an assessment coordinator to manipulate data, integrate data with other data sources (e.g., survey), recode data elements, and generate some forms of numeric reporting.

An example of using a data extraction tool to integrate multiple data sets would be to extract biographical and demographic student information from a campus-wide data resource, add student participation data on large-scale first-year programs throughout the year to the database structure, and then at the end of the year extract and add student retention and academic performance data into the database. The product in this example would be to explore possible relationships among student input characteristics, engagement in first-year programs, retention, and academic performance metrics.

Spreadsheet applications such as Microsoft Excel and Quattro Pro also have the ability to link to external data sources in order to obtain information for later analysis. Although spreadsheets are not as powerful as databases in terms of data integration and organization of information, they are excellent applications for data sorting, numerical reporting, and coding qualitative information. Spreadsheets are designed to be easier to navigate than databases and data extraction tools. In addition, spreadsheets are already available on a personal computing platform.

Training and cost are significant considerations in terms of product selection for a data extraction tool. For this reason, it is good practice to research what data extraction tool is the most commonly adopted across campus, as personnel have already learned to use the software and could assist with training and expertise.

Types of Assessment Tools: A Review of Software Types

The following sections review the major types of software and how they can be used to manipulate, analyze, and report key research findings.

Databases: Powerful, Multipurpose Applications

In addition to their usefulness in data extraction, databases such as Microsoft Access are useful platforms to organize and manipulate information for a variety of business purposes. In the 1980s and 1990s, enterprise resource programs (ERPs) were typically devoted to supporting common university-wide applications, such as admissions, financial aid, registrar's office proceedings, and billing. During that time, smaller-scale business processes, such as new student orientation, on-campus housing, and student conduct records, were transforming from paper-based systems into locally developed database applications. From a business process perspective, databases at that time were designed to organize, manipulate, and generate reports that supported each business process need, such as residence hall rosters, damage reports, student conduct reports, and orientation session rosters.

In today's context, databases still are designed and enhanced to meet business process requirements but can also be designed to meet the data needs of assessment coordinators. From that perspective, databases can be used to extract data from other systems, integrate that data with other assessment data such as surveys, export integrated data sets to statistical analysis software, and provide some basic reporting capabilities. Databases are also useful in recoding data.

Although databases have powerful organization and descriptive numeric reporting functionality, they are somewhat limited in terms of analyzing data using inferential analysis testing and in producing graphics. Selecting which database to use for assessment purposes depends on the level of training that would be needed to run the application, the costs associated with its use, and the level of adoption that application has on the campus. It would make some sense for the assessment coordinator to adopt a database application that is perceived as the campus standard in order to take part in site license discounts, centralized training, and identifying local campus expertise in using the application. Database applications often exist as part of an office suite containing not only the database but also word processing, spreadsheet, and presentation software for little to no additional cost to the assessment coordinator.

Spreadsheets: Versatile, Multipurpose Tools

Although databases are powerful data extraction, integration, and organization tools, spreadsheets are powerful in their own right in numeric manipulation and numeric and graphical reporting. Spreadsheet applications such as Microsoft Excel and Quattro Pro are designed to allow users to view, recode, transform, summarize, and report numeric variables both descriptively and inferentially to a lesser degree.

Spreadsheets are organized cells of rows and columns. For example, a row may represent a survey respondent, a column a particular question, and a cell the value for a given response for that given question. The first row is usually reserved for the column heading description such as "Question One." Spreadsheets are useful in quickly performing numeric calculations and copying those calculations to other items.

The statistical analysis capabilities of spreadsheets have grown beyond descriptive data calculations to include inferential analysis and other complex mathematical treatments. Advanced help topics and "wizard" features can assist the assessment coordinator in tasks ranging from developing regression analysis modeling of survey data to determining amortization (loan repayment) schedules for a new car.

Spreadsheets can also be used to organize and report data in a form that is ready for presentation. Once calculated, the finished table might look something like Table 5.1.

For formal presentation or reporting purposes, spreadsheets are able to transform a table like Table 5.1 into various types of easy-to-generate graphic representations (e.g., bar graph, line graph, pie chart, etc.), including titles and labels in addition to adding color and other textual effects to the tables themselves.

A good assessment reporting practice is to summarize results in three ways—numerically, graphically, and narratively—to reflect the three different learning styles of the intended audience. As one can see from Table 5.1, spreadsheets can be used to readily generate both numeric and graphic representations of the assessment data being analyzed.

The decision to acquire a particular spreadsheet application follows the same principles that were suggested with database applications, namely, level of training, costs associated with use, and level of adoption that the application has on the campus. As with databases, spreadsheet applications often exist as a part of a larger office suite with other useful software types for little to no additional cost to the assessment coordinator.

Table 5.1   **Simple Calculations Example**

Question Number	Male	Female	Average (mean) (calculated values)
Q2	3.78	4.23	4.01
Q3	2.94	3.45	3.20
Q4	3.25	2.95	3.10

Statistical Analysis Software: The Workhorse Tool

Database and spreadsheet software provide some numeric analysis and reporting capabilities, but they largely involve basic descriptive analysis with little in the way of inferential analysis. Here is where the use of statistical analysis software such as SPSS, SAS, and SYSTAT becomes an important and integral part of the work of an assessment coordinator. Reporting on assessment findings often consists of more than citing descriptive numbers such as counts, frequency distributions, and mean scores. The assessment coordinator may wish to also study the results in greater detail by using inferential analysis techniques to determine if those descriptive numbers are significantly different in a statistical sense. Conducting inferential analyses often adds a sense of "what's really important" to the assessment findings.

To display data, statistical analysis software uses the same row and column system used in spreadsheets. A column is called a field or variable in statistical analysis software data sets, and a row is referred to as a record. An additional layer of field or variable description called labels is available in statistical analysis software and can be used for visual reporting.

Statistical analysis software is adept at quickly recoding data, and, unlike spreadsheets, it allows multiple analyses for different groups of data to be run in one operation. For example, the level of significance tests across all variables would be run once with the option of displaying graphical representations of each test alongside the numeric output. Thinking back to the good practice of reporting assessment findings in three ways (numerically, graphically, and narratively), using statistical analysis software can in effect kill two of the three reporting birds with one stone.

The quality of statistical analysis software program user interfaces varies between vendors. SAS, for example, typically requires the user to manually type commands to select the data to be examined, the tests to run, output parameters to be reported. This allows the user to be very precise in defining what data are to be examined, how they are to be examined, and what information is to be displayed at the end of the analysis. However, it also requires some level of additional training to learn the specific syntax terms needed to run the analysis. Both SYSTAT and SPSS have extensive graphical user interfaces that minimize but do not eliminate the need to understand the underlying command syntax in order to conduct an analysis. Having a well-designed graphical user interface simplifies the actual process of running an analysis; however, the assessment coordinator must still understand, based on the data he or she has and the assessment or research methodology he or she wishes to apply, why a certain type of analysis should be chosen.

Statistical analysis software programs also have the ability to extract data directly from other data systems and to integrate data from multiple data sources. Depending on the software selected and type of data sources that exist on campus, this could reduce or even eliminate the need for separate data extraction and database tools. Statistical analysis software programs often serve a multipurpose, workhorse role.

Given the complexity, varied feature sets, and the needs of the assessment coordinator, the suggestions for acquiring a statistical analysis software program are similar to those of data extraction. Generally, training and cost are the most significant issues in terms of product selection. As in the case of data extraction tools, it may be a good idea to research what data extraction tool is the most commonly adopted by the campus community as faculty and staff members have already learned to use the software and could assist with training and share their expertise as needed.

Word Processing: Narrative Reporting and Other Assessment Functions

As mentioned in a previous section, a good assessment report is a blend of all three representations: narrative, numeric, and graphical. The immediately previous sections have addressed the use of tools to generate numeral and graphics-based information needed within an assessment report or presentation. Narrative reporting is less of a technology issue than it is a writing-style issue. There are any number of assessment writing styles, all of which vary according to the skill of the writer, the intended audience, and the type of information being presented. Schuh (2009) detailed a four-step process that could be useful to an assessment coordinator seeking to develop a final report or presentation. The four steps include the following:

1. Identify the audience for the report.
2. Develop appropriate formats for the report.
3. Identify the components of the report.
4. Identify recommendations for practice. (p. 173)

One can see where the written (narrative) aspects of the report can provide the framework for the larger work, which, especially in steps two and three, can also incorporate numeric and graphic output.

Related to word processing software is the introduction of supplemental programs such as voice recognition. One such product released in July 2014 claims an accuracy level of up to 99% right out of the box (Nuance.com, 2014). This type of product has the potential for quickly transcribing handwritten notes from assessment activities such as focus groups and case study conversations into written text. Those data can then be imported into a spreadsheet and recoded to group common themes together for subsequent analysis. This type of capability could be useful in certain types of qualitative research settings, such as the World Café method (World Café, 2014) where data in written form are obtained from large-scale audiences around a common set of focused topics. This type of approach can generate many pages of written comments and quotes. Handwritten audience feedback can be quickly and accurately transcribed into text by the use of voice recognition software and then analyzed via the recoding method described earlier.

Some voice recognition software can also be used to translate written text to speech and then recorded. This feature could be useful when sharing research findings with the visually impaired. The word processing software application used by the assessment coordinator for these functions is largely a matter of personal choice or perhaps is a university-wide adoption via a low-cost site license. The assessment coordinator needs to make certain that the word processing software selected has the feature sets he or she needs to write the narrative component of assessment reports and to provide other assessment support activities via supportive software.

Graphic Output Reporting

Generating graphic representations of numeric data for reporting purposes can be accomplished through many different types of tools, including, but not limited to, spreadsheets, statistical analysis software, database programs, and data analytics software.

Selecting the right tools for producing narrative, numeric, graphic representations of data for reporting purposes should be based on the types of data that are collected and analyzed and what types of reports are requested by the departments with whom the data coordinator is working. As these applications continue to evolve and advance in increasing sophistication, additional features of the other types of software are being incorporated. Database programs and statistical analysis programs have recently evolved to include producing graphic representations of the data, and some spreadsheet programs are now able to access external data sources. This is a significant merging of functionality that continues to increase over time and perhaps will enable the selection of just one tool in the future to perform functions that up until now have required multiple software applications.

A final aspect of reporting entails the recent development of data visualization tools as a means of summarizing key findings in simple ways using a combination of short narrative statements, key numeric information, and simple graphic representations of the data to be shared. For example, a division annual report executive summary is typically a one- or two-page narrative description of key activities or findings. Data visualization applications can transform those narratives into multiple brief indicators, often referred to as infographics or information graphics, of each significant activity or finding. The use of key performance indicators is a good example of information that can be transformed using data visualization tools into effective executive summaries that are largely nonnarrative. One of the more common places for these applications to exist currently are cloud-based solutions like Tableau. These data visualization tools have the ability to transform traditionally narrative and complex research studies and annual reports into a digestible format that can be easily understood by a wider audience. For more information about the use of data visualization tools in student affairs organizations, use the search strings "data visualization student affairs" or "data visualization software" in a search engine.

Presenting Data

Earlier sections in this chapter have discussed tools and practices that are needed to prepare assessment information in multiple forms (numeric, graphic, and narrative) for reporting purposes; the tools needed to present a well-crafted final product are just as important. Assessment coordinators should give careful thought to how they present their findings to an intended audience. For some purposes, a narrative report with a brief executive summary would suffice; whereas, for others, a visually engaging and informative presentation would be the best way to convey assessment findings. This breadth and depth of reporting types may require presentation layer software that enables the assessment coordinator to display his or her findings in an organized and graphically appealing manner. Probably two of the most used products in this category are PowerPoint and Keynote. Both products allow for the creation of slides that can be used by the assessment coordinator to craft a presentation that can incorporate text, numeric information, and graphic representations of data in order to build a compelling presentation. A more recently developed cloud-based product, Prezi, contains many of the same features of the previous two products but adds powerful and more meaningful graphic transitions between slides, enables group collaboration, and is mobile device friendly. At this time, however, Prezi is not compatible with most screen readers, so is not accessible to audiences with visual needs.

Although presentation layer tools are important for developing effective and engaging reports, other types of software tools have been developed that can be used to convey information in a variety of forms. Mentioned briefly in the previous section, a commonly used term to describe this software genre is *infographics*, which is short for information graphics. Infographic tools can take on a wide variety of forms. One such tool, Wordle, can tabulate, summarize, and display narrative data from sources such as department mission and vision statements as word pictures with variable-size text depending on how often a word appears in the core document. The more often a word is used, the larger it appears in the word cloud. Infographic tools can also be used to organize assessment data and build objects that can incorporate numeric, graphic, and narrative data into new forms. This functionality, often termed *data visualization*, includes software such as Tableau, Cognos, and Piktochart. These tools are increasingly used for drafting annual reports, generating key performance indicators, and summarizing key survey results. In terms of acquiring one or more of these tools, factors such as cost, level of complexity, training required, accessibility to users with visual and other disabilities, and ease of use are all important to consider.

Future Developments

As the profession and technology continue to evolve, so do the techniques and purposes for using technology in assessment. While it is always a challenge to predict technology development, there are two emerging trends at this time that are important to keep in mind. The first is the growing use of social media by students and institutions and how these platforms can become tools to assist with data collection. The second is the idea of "big data" and how to best cultivate and use large data sources in planning and improvement.

Emergence of Social Networking Media

After the advent of Facebook in 2004 (Phillips, 2007), college-age students flocked to this new genre of technology to build and share an online presence, communicate with friends, share photos, and provide commentary on topics ranging from their daily activity to world events. Estimates vary on college student use of Facebook based on the audience sample and time frame. One recent publication cited that Facebook was used by 88.6% of 18- to 24-year-olds in November 2013, which was down from 91.5% in February 2013 (McDermott, 2014).

Since Facebook, other platforms have emerged, including Twitter, Instagram, Tumblr, Snapchat, YouTube, Vine, WordPress, and Yik Yak. All these platforms enable some form of digital communication and information sharing among users. Although the use and audience of these tools has grown significantly to include virtually all age groups and administrative and departmental users within the higher education sector, it is clear that the college-age population is using most of these tools with increasing frequency (McDermott, 2014). Given the rich degree of communication and content that can be found within these systems, what role can social media play for the assessment coordinator?

Social media and online tools such as PhotoVoice provide an opportunity to expand traditional data collection methods such as document analysis, visual methods, and, especially, photo journaling. Many of these tools can take what used to be a resource-intensive data collection project and transform it into something more accessible to students and the organization collecting data.

However, Martinez-Aleman (2014) cautioned that there are regulatory, legal, Americans with Disabilities Act, Family Educational Rights and Privacy Act, and copyright issues that need to be taken into account when considering utilizing these tools for assessment and accountability purposes. That said, social media use represents a rich opportunity for the assessment coordinator to explore student-to-student and student-to-organization communication and engagement patterns, to quantify and address timely topical concerns, and to provide feedback mechanisms to students relative to programs and services without the need for targeted surveys. As part of a leadership program, students are asked to blog their reflections from various service activities, workshops, and mentorship experience. An office of student leadership could then use those blogs to track individual student progress and also identify progress toward learning outcomes or gaps in learning. Another potential use could be an analysis of student feedback posted on a department Facebook page in response to a question prompt or, at a base level, student commentary on a new program or policy. These examples would require careful monitoring of the selected social media tool and in some cases involve recoding a large number of responses to summarize common student concerns.

Social networking media will continue to evolve based on changes in technology, mobile devices, and perceived needs. Like the other tools mentioned in this chapter, it will be critically important for the assessment coordinator to include this tool in his or her professional development activities.

Analytics and Tackling Big Data

For the purpose of this discussion, the term *data analytics* is loosely defined as a process that integrates information from multiple data sources. The integrated information is then analyzed using advanced statistical techniques for purposes beyond simple reporting. This process is a very recent development primarily used in the business sector to analyze large amounts of disparate sets of data in an effort to assist the business in identifying new issues and adopting new business practices to address discovered obstacles. At present these more complex processes are not typically in the domain of the assessment coordinator, but some of the advanced tool sets are beginning to be introduced into statistical analysis software. As such it may be in the assessment coordinator's best interest to learn how these new tools and techniques can be applied to a university or student affairs setting.

Looking at higher education, it may be possible to develop future research models where university information across the enterprise is purposefully captured, integrated, and analyzed to determine comprehensive models of student achievement, student departure, and comprehensive time-to-degree studies. Existing data such as student surveys, new student orientation, social engagement variables, and out-of-class involvement housed within student affairs organization could be easily incorporated into these studies.

Historically, a large part of assessment work involved reporting descriptive statistics based on levels of student engagement, student satisfaction and needs surveys, learning outcomes, and perhaps a few national survey efforts. The tools were less complex, easier to navigate, and required less conceptual and technical training than what may be required in today's assessment environment. In the near future, assessment coordinators may be expected to conduct advanced inferential analyses on multiple sources of data for a variety of purposes, including the impact of student affairs programs on academic success, retention, and time to degree. Other possibilities are assessing student learning outcomes, student skill development, and determining the impact of participation on academic and social engagement. Thille et al. (2014) investigate the concept of so-called learner logs in a data-enriched assessment environment. Students log their process as they learn and work through assignments. Thille et al. stated,

> One of the most generally applicable results of this research has been to demonstrate the tremendous potential towards better assessment that comes from digital logs of how learners work through assignments, as opposed to just the learner's final submission. (p. 9)

The tool sets and conceptual knowledge required for these types of studies continue to expand as the ability to analyze increasingly complex data sets emerges.

It is important to note that the level of analysis and use of findings requires knowledge of applications that typically are not part of graduate preparation programs and are more sophisticated than a typical assessment coordinator's education at the present time.

Conclusion

Schuh (2009) indicated in his publication *Assessment Methods for Student Affairs* that upgrading assessment skills will become a growth industry to make certain "that student affairs practitioners are able to conduct assessments at an acceptable level" (p. 243). This holds especially true of assessment coordinators as the assessment models they may be expected to generate increase in complexity. In order to stay current, it will be imperative that assessment coordinators continue to advance their knowledge and professional development surrounding these advanced tools and future research models by attending workshops and vendor presentations and by networking with leaders in this field.

Although this chapter focuses heavily on the use of technological tools in assessment activities, the interactions with colleagues in need of expertise, with data owners as partners in assessment activities, and with peers and supervisors in need of assessment findings will be the primary focus of the assessment coordinator. Mastery of the myriad of assessment tools is essential, but assessment coordinators, like their fellow student affairs professionals, should continue to remain focused on assessment for enhancing student learning and promoting student success.

References

Auguste, B., Cota, A., Jayaram, K., & Laboissiere, M. (2010). *Winning by degrees: The strategies of highly productive higher-education institutions.* Retrieved from mckinseyonsociety.com/winning-by-degrees

Chickering, A., & Ehrmann, S. (1996). Implementing the seven principles: Technology as a lever. *AAHE Bulletin,* 3–6.

Chickering, A., & Gamson, Z. (1987). Seven principles for good practice in undergraduate education. *AAHE Bulletin,* March, 307.

Davenport, T. H., & Harris, J. G. (2007). *Competing on analytics.* Cambridge, MA: Harvard Business School Press.

Dillman, D. A. (1978). *Mail and telephone surveys: The total design method.* New York, NY: Wiley and Sons.

Elling, T. W., & Brown, S. J. (2001). Advancing technology and student affairs practice. In R. B. Winston Jr., D. G. Creamer, & T. K. Miller (Eds.), *The professional student affairs administrator: Education, leader, and manager* (pp. 81–104). New York, NY: Taylor & Francis.

Guidry, K. R. (2012). *Ongoing research into student affairs technology history.* Retrieved from mistakengoal.com/blog/category/student-affairs/naspa/

Katz, S. N. (2001). In information technology, don't mistake a tool for a goal. *Chronicle of Higher Education, 47*(40). Retrieved from www.princeton.edu/~snkatz/papers/CHE_6-15-01.html

Macfadyen, L. P., Dawson, S., Pardo, A., & Gasevic, D. (2014). Embracing big data in complex educational systems: The learning analytics imperative and the policy challenge. *Research & Practice in Assessment, 9*(2), 17–28.

Martinez-Aleman, A. (2014). Social media go to college. *Change Magazine,* January–February. Retrieved from www.changemag.org/Archives/Back%20Issues/2014/January-February%202014/socialmedia_full.html

McDermott, J. (2014, January 21). Facebook losing its edge among college-aged adults. *Digiday.* Retrieved from digiday.com/platforms/social-platforms-college-kids-now-prefer

Nichols, J. O. (1995). Assessment planning. In J. O. Nichols (Ed.), *A practitioner's handbook for institutional effectiveness and student outcomes assessment implementation* (pp. 123–137). New York, NY: Agathon.

Nuance.com. (2014). *Dragon naturallyspeaking 13 professional data sheet.* Retrieved from www.nuance.com/ucmprod/groups/dragon/@web-enus/documents/collateral/nc_033978.pdf

Phillips, S. (2007, July 25). A brief history of Facebook. *Guardian.* Retrieved from www.theguardian.com/technology/2007/jul/25/media.newmedia

Saunders, K. & Wohlgemuth, D. R. (2009). Using existing databases. In J. H. Schuh (Ed.), *Assessment methods for student affairs* (pp. 23–50). San Francisco, CA: Jossey-Bass

Schuh, J. H. (Ed.). (2009). *Assessment methods for student affairs.* San Francisco, CA: Jossey-Bass.

Thille, C., Schneider, D. E., Kizilcec, R. F., Piech, C., Halawa, S. A., & Greene, D. K. (2014). The future of data-enriched assessment. *Research & Practice in Assessment, 9*(2), 5–16.

U.S. Department of Education. (2010). *Transforming American education: Learning powered by technology.* Retrieved from https://www.ed.gov/sites/default/files/NETP-2010-final-report.pdf

World Café. (2014, November 24). *World Café method.* Retrieved from www.theworldcafe.com

6

Tenet Six: Building Talent and Increasing Assessment Knowledge

Vicki L. Wise
Robert W. Aaron

AN ESSENTIAL element in building assessment talent and increasing assessment capacity is increasing the number of people who have the time, skills, and knowledge to conduct effective assessment projects. Staff members throughout the division must have the ability to contribute to assessment efforts. One person, or even a small team, can neither design nor implement an assessment framework in isolation. All division staff members need to be empowered and educated on how to develop this framework and generate evidence. Therefore, one important role of the assessment coordinator is to assess the varying skill levels that already exist throughout the division and work to build that talent through formal and informal learning opportunities. This chapter explores how to help staff members develop assessment skills and build knowledge needed to build a systemic and sustainable assessment program.

Often when student affairs professionals struggle to implement effective assessment in their divisions, it is because of a departmental lack of knowledge or skill set. Bresciani, Gardner, and Hickmott (2010) reported that the main barriers to effective outcomes-based assessment were lack of time and resources for professional development, lack of knowledge and skills for conducting assessment, and lack of a framework for integrating assessment into practice and collaborating with faculty in this process. Moreover, staff members often experience unease and mistrust in the assessment process, not knowing expectations from leadership and how assessment results will be used. Many of these barriers can be overcome through building communities of talent where staff members have access to assessment structures and education. In general, though, to begin this process of eliminating barriers, it is essential to remove some of the anxiety around assessment by reinforcing its intended use for program improvement and measurement of student learning, not for personnel evaluation. It is also essential to designate one staff member to coordinate assessment efforts. This coordinator cannot work in isolation, however. Initially the assessment coordinator carries the load for "doing" assessment, but the core mission of the assessment coordinator is to develop the capacity of student affairs staff to conduct assessment independently (Student Affairs Leadership Council, 2009). Increasing assessment knowledge is an ongoing process requiring maintenance to "boost" people up from year to year to add to their skill set. When this is accomplished, the division's assessment efforts as a whole become stronger and more robust each year.

Both seasoned and new professionals vary in their graduate preparation in assessment training. Although student affairs professionals entering the field within the past decade often have had some degree of classroom training in assessment techniques and applications in student affairs administration, it is more likely that their midlevel and senior counterparts may not ever have had hands-on experience or formal training with assessment until they had been in their leadership roles for several years. Building assessment skills needs to be approached from many angles: "up," "out," "across," and "down." For each level in the organization, the up, out, across, and down views may look different. For example, a senior student affairs officer (SSAO) needs to know how to use the data to express details of the student experience upward to other top-level university administrators, outward to potential donors or other external stakeholders, across the traditional academic/student affairs divide in order to develop new partnerships around the college or university, and downward to staff to instill the importance of using data to inform decision making as evidence of impact on student learning and engagement. It is essential for SSAOs to be successful at communicating results in multiple directions so that they can champion the work of assessment in their division and communicate results in various ways to a wide variety of constituent groups.

Whereas SSAOs should have a broad knowledge of how assessment works in student affairs, directors of functional student affairs departments should have deeper knowledge of assessment beyond communicating results. Directors need to oversee the planning, prioritizing, or providing direction for assessment efforts in their functional areas. In addition, they need to understand various issues around collecting, analyzing, reporting, and using results for improvement. Moreover, as their staff members are often charged with conducting assessment, directors need to support the professional development of their staff and allocate time and resources to further assessment efforts.

Staff members in these functional areas, therefore, need to have competency with basic assessment skills, while receiving support from the division's assessment coordinator. They should have some basic knowledge, as outlined by the ACPA/NASPA Competencies (American College Personnel Association & National Association of Student Personnel Administrators Joint Task Force on Professional Competencies Standards, 2010), in data collection techniques and basic data analysis so as to develop a common understanding of issues across various student interventions. Ultimately, the staff, directors, and SSAOs must collaborate regularly in order to paint the full picture of the student experience based on a systematic manner of collecting results. Assessment skills will vary across different levels of the division, but all levels contribute to creating programs and services that support learning for a wide variety of students at our institutions.

It is crucial, therefore, to focus on building assessment skills throughout the student affairs organization in order to collectively raise the bar of competency for assessment. The assessment coordinator can further the professional development for assessment skills with resources such as the Assessment Skills and Knowledge standards from ACPA (American College Personnel Association, 2007) or the NASPA Assessment, Evaluation, and Research Knowledge Community (AERKC), in addition to the assessment competencies from the ACPA/NASPA task force (2010). The remainder of this chapter explores a variety of ideas for building assessment attitudes, skills, and knowledge, thus fostering sound professional development across the organization.

How to Build Assessment Talent and Knowledge

A new assessment coordinator's first step should be a conversation with leadership to get clarity around expectations for ongoing assessment in the division. Senior student affairs leaders need to convey the importance of conducting assessment and require that all departments participate in assessment (Student Affairs Leadership Council, 2009). Following discussions with leadership, it is then essential for the assessment coordinator to alleviate any misunderstandings staff members may have about assessment. Staff members benefit from understanding that the value of assessment is to gain a better understanding of how student affairs programs and services affect students' knowledge, skills, and attitudes. Services (such as registration and records, financial aid, housing, and student legal services, to name a few) may not view assessment as essential or applicable to their work, especially as it relates to student learning. Moreover, as stated earlier, reassuring staff members that assessment is for program improvement and not for personnel evaluation helps alleviate any misgivings about conducting assessment. Other misgivings staff members may hold about assessment may be more related to the time, expertise, and support needed. Thus, the assessment coordinator can alleviate some of these concerns by assuring staff members that the coordinator will oversee the learning opportunities to empower them with the assessment expertise they need, and that training will occur in myriad ways and at a variety of times to accommodate the time constraints they often face.

The assessment coordinator's determination of assessment trainings and information needs can be viewed through a lens similar to the one used for building capacity: upward, outward, across, and down. Top-level administrators typically speak with colleagues outside student affairs who serve in other leadership roles, such as academic deans, faculty, or other administrators over large shops like human resources or budgeting and planning. With all external audiences, it is essential for the SSAOs to have a handle on data that describe the student experience in terms of how they learn and are otherwise supported outside the classroom. Midlevel managers such as departmental directors tend to communicate with audiences both internal and external to student affairs. Internally, since they may act as decision makers to improve direct services to students, they often address fellow staff members or students directly with results from a variety of assessments. In addition, many directors serve on university-wide committees and represent the division to these external constituents. Similar to the SSAO, midlevel professionals must be prepared to represent student learning to many external voices, many of which are actively working with students in a variety of ways. Often, assessment results shared at the midlevel must be actionable results used for making decisions to improve the student experience. Staff members, ultimately, are responsible for conducting assessment of their programs and services, so they must be able to engage in all aspects of the assessment process.

In all cases and at all levels, it is important to consider where division members are starting from in their assessment knowledge and experiences. Conducting a needs assessment assists the coordinator in developing suitable training. The American College Personnel Association's *Assessment Skills and Knowledge: Content Standards for Student Affairs Practitioners and Scholars (ASK)* (2007) and *Professional Competency Areas for Student Affairs Practitioners: Rubrics for Professional Development* (n.d.) are great resources to establish baseline competency and training needs. The ASK standards describe assessment skills and knowledge areas appropriate for all student affairs practitioners. The professional competencies then operationalize those areas of knowledge and skills into tangible tasks for staff to be able to perform at beginner, intermediate, and advanced levels. Both documents can be used in a variety of ways to assess staff skills and competencies for assessment. Once gap areas are established, then assessment coordinators can focus training needs for specific groups to fill these knowledge gaps and bring most key staff members to a common competency level for assessment across the division.

When assessing staff competencies, the assessment coordinator needs to simultaneously establish an infrastructure to support assessment. One way to form a foundation for the infrastructure is creating an assessment council composed of staff members at differing levels of competency. This can be a helpful tool for developing a collaborative culture around division-wide assessment issues, assessing competency across colleagues, and providing information to the assessment coordinator on current issues for which data can be used for making decisions. Establishing an infrastructure allows for shared language, processes, and procedures that are part of developing and then sustaining assessment talent and capacity. There are several ways to create a shared understanding of assessment, and it is essential to have a variety of staff members involved in the process.

The following strategies help lay the foundation for assessment by clarifying what assessment practice means, how staff members conduct assessment, and how to report on it in systematic ways.

Share a Common Language Through a Dictionary of Terms

Developing a common language around assessment is essential to begin the process, and the aforementioned assessment committee can be used to communicate that language division-wide. Nuances in terminology have often kept staff from understanding and doing assessment. As there are a variety of methods for conducting assessment, it is important for a division to establish a common language to ensure all staff members are on the same page. Many institutions provide glossaries of commonly used assessment terms. The division of enrollment management and student affairs at Portland State University has a searchable glossary of terms created by their assessment council. The division of student affairs at the University of Kentucky has a glossary that explains what assessment is and provides links to other universities with glossaries. James Madison University's Center for Assessment and Research Studies has an extensive, searchable database of assessment terms with citations for each term. The student affairs assessment team at the University of Wisconsin at Milwaukee has provided a plethora of online assessment tools, including their student affairs page with the sound advice, "Don't get stuck in assessment jargon!" Their vocabulary list provides definitions for commonly used assessment terms. There are many more sites to access and use so the assessment coordinator and teams do not have to develop a glossary in house:

- James Madison University: people.jmu.edu/yangsx
- Oregon State University: oregonstate.edu/studentaffairs/sites/ default/files/docs/Assessment_Handbook_2006.pdf
- Portland State University: www.pdx.edu/sites/www.pdx.edu .studentaffairs/files/PSUStudentAffairsTerminology.pdf
- The Ohio State University: cssl.osu.edu/resources1/conduc ting-assessment
- University of Kentucky: www.uky.edu/StudentAffairs/Assess ment/glossary.html

- University of Wisconsin at Milwaukee: uwm.edu/saassess
ment/toolkit/vocabulary

Develop a Handbook of Assessment Practice

Typically, a division's assessment handbook covers five key areas of conducting assessment—setting goals, analyzing data, analyzing findings, reporting, and using results for improvement—supplemented by specific examples from past assessment projects in that division. The handbook serves as a guide to enable numerous staff members across a division to conduct the basic principles of assessment until the assessment coordinator or assessment committee can help with more advanced needs. For example, Portland State University's Student Affairs Assessment Council created a best practice assessment handbook to provide a common language and structure for their assessment practice, as they examine the unique ways in which they contribute to student learning and development. The handbook includes a visual display of their assessment cycle and detailed information about how to delve deeper into parts of the assessment cycle. Staff members use this resource to guide their assessment practice.

Several other universities provide handbooks/guides for assessment practice. For example, The Ohio State University Center for the Study of Student Life's webpage "Conducting Assessment" offers visuals and plans for components of an assessment plan and progression of an assessment project that outlines the steps of an assessment project. Oregon State University has an assessment handbook that includes developing an assessment plan and the components of an assessment plan, as well as taking the reader through all phases of the assessment cycle. Other sites with extensive handbooks include Weber State University's division of student affairs, University of Iowa's division of student life, and Gallaudet University's office of student assessment, to name a few. Again, the assessment coordinator does not need to create a handbook from scratch when there are so many great resources available.

- Gallaudet University: www.gallaudet.edu/Documents/assess
ment_handbook.pdf

- Oregon State University: oregonstate.edu/studentaffairs/sites/default/files/docs/Assessment_Handbook_2006.pdf
- Portland State University: www.pdx.edu/studentaffairs/assessment-planning-and-practice
- The Ohio State University: cssl.osu.edu/resources1/conducting-assessment/
- University of Iowa: vp.studentlife.uiowa.edu/assets/Updated-Assessment-Handbook.pdf
- Weber State University: www.weber.edu/wsuimages/SAAssessment/assessmenthandbook.pdf

Develop Common Templates for Assessment Planning

Having programs report their assessment plans in cohesive ways allows the assessment coordinator to know at a glance where programs are in their assessment implementation. A well-developed assessment plan should follow whichever assessment cycle is being used and typically contains the following areas: developing goals; measurable program and learning outcomes; assessment methods to measure outcomes; a plan for program implementation and data collection time frame; a plan to analyze, interpret, report, and use results; and a plan to disseminate results to stakeholders and provide feedback to participants.

The following are several examples of assessment templates from a variety of institutions around the country:

- Ball State University: cms.bsu.edu/about/administrativeoffices/studentaffairs/studentaffairsassessmentplan
- Boston College: www.bc.edu/content/dam/files/offices/vpsa/pdf/app2014.pdf
- Indiana State University: www.indstate.edu/studentaffairsresearch/Library.htm
- Oregon State University: oregonstate.edu/studentaffairs/assessment-formats-and-examples
- University of California–San Diego: studentresearch.ucsd.edu/_files/assessment/workshops/2012-10-12_how-to-develop-your-assessment-plan-handouts.pdf

- University of Houston: www.uh.edu/dsa/about_student_affairs
  /assessment_planning/forms.html

Develop Common Templates for Annual Reporting

An annual report portfolio is a great way to centralize reporting
in the division. In this portfolio each department would use the
same template for reporting on their progress in meeting their goals
for the current year and setting goals for the year ahead. Portland
State University's division of enrollment management and student
affairs is in the fourth year of using a portfolio for annual reporting.
Their departments report their mission, vision, and values;
a year in review of their goals; and their future goals. The Ohio
State University's Office of Student Life developed a web-based
system that houses all annual reporting data. Department assessment coordinators can log in to the system and provide a variety
of resources in the annual report, from completed assessment projects to plans for the following year. Many of these portfolios are
internal-use-only sites, and thus are password protected, so contact
an institution to see if it will share a copy of the site that could
be modified for your institution. In addition, many sites now use
briefing books for condensed annual reporting and to showcase programs and services annually. Briefing books are concise, typically
no more than two pages, and highlight areas of student affairs. One
could think of them as a marketing tool for student affairs. Many
campuses have adopted briefing books for their annual reporting.
Following are just a few institutions with examples of student affairs
briefing books online:

- Alfred University: www.alfred.edu/students/admin.cfm
- Carleton College: apps.carleton.edu/campus/dos/assets/Stude
  nt_Life_Briefing_Book_2013.pdf
- College of the Holy Cross: offices.holycross.edu/sites/all/modul
  es/tinytinymce/tinymce/jscripts/tiny_mce/plugins/filemanager/
  files/studentaffairs/sabriefingbookletweb.pdf
- Stony Brook University: studentaffairs.stonybrook.edu/stu/sto
  ry/briefing_book.shtml

- University at Albany, State University of New York: www.albany
  .edu/studentsuccess/assessment/BriefingBook/BriefingBook
  _2014/Briefing%20Book%202013-14.pdf

Once shared understanding of terminology and assessment processes and reporting are in place, the assessment coordinator can
then develop (or gather) resources, tools, and trainings to build and
support sustainable assessment competencies and practice. There
are multitude ways to build assessment competencies; some can be
developed in house, and many resources from other institutions and
professional organizations may be used. The resources provided in
this section are not an exhaustive list, but they are more than sufficient for any assessment program.

Adopt or Develop an Assessment Tool Kit

An assessment tool kit contains the tools staff members need to
conduct assessment. A great example comes from the National
Institute for Learning Outcomes Assessment (NILOA). NILOA provides information on tools that universities and colleges use for the
assessment of student learning such as tests, surveys, portfolios, and
curriculum mapping. In addition, the Student Affairs Assessment
Leaders (SAAL) organization is a great resource in which leaders
of assessment nationally contribute to assessment learning through
their repositories of assessment resources and online conversations
via their electronic mailing lists. Many student affairs assessment
websites and professional organizations provide access to information on selecting and using a variety of assessment tools, including
those sites listed previously.

- Christopher Newport University: cnu.edu/assessment/resour
  ces/
- NILOA: www.learningoutcomeassessment.org/ToolKit.html
- North Carolina State University: assessment.dasa.ncsu.edu/
  forms-and-assessment-resources-dasa
- SAAL: studentaffairsassessment.org/assessment-resources
- Texas A&M: assessment.tamu.edu/resources/resources_index
  .html

- University of Arizona: www.studentaffairs.arizona.edu/assess ment/toolbox_toolkits.php
- University of California–San Diego: studentresearch.ucsd.edu/ assessment/toolkit/index.html

Provide Access to an Assessment Library

The NILOA site also provides access to publications, assessment resources, and links to assessment websites at a number of higher education institutions. The Ohio State University's Center for the Study of Student Life has a wide variety of resources on its website designed to help others build assessment skills. In addition, it offers a set of webinars to guide others through common data analysis procedures that many assessment professionals use on a regular basis. There are numerous student affairs websites that offer access to online research and articles. What is notable across these sites is the listing of assessment books considered seminal works in student affairs assessment. Every assessment coordinator needs to purchase and share the books listed here as a start to engaging in assessment practice with student affairs staff:

- Bresciani, M. J., Gardner, M. M., & Hickmott, J. (2010). *Demonstrating student success: A practical guide to outcomes-based assessment of learning and development in student affairs.* Sterling, VA: Stylus.
- Bresciani, M. J., Zelna, C. L., & Anderson, J. A. (2004). *Assessing student learning and development: A handbook for practitioners.* Washington, DC: National Association of Student Personnel Administrators.
- Council for the Advancement of Standards in Higher Education. (2015). *CAS professional standards for higher education* (9th ed.). Washington, DC: Council for the Advancement of Standards in Higher Education.
- Schuh, J. M., & Associates. (2009). *Assessment methods for student affairs.* San Francisco: Jossey-Bass.
- Schuh, J. M., Upcraft, M. L., & Associates. (2001). *Assessment practice in student affairs: An applications manual.* San Francisco: Jossey-Bass.

- Suskie, L. A. (2009). *Assessing student learning: A common sense guide* (2nd ed.). San Francisco: Jossey-Bass.
- Yousey-Elsener, K. M. (2013). *Successful assessment in student affairs: A how-to guide*. Little Falls, NJ: PaperClip Communications.

The following sites, in addition to many sites previously mentioned, also offer great resources for recommended readings in assessment.

- NASPA: www.naspa.org/constituent-groups/kcs/assessment -evaluation-and-research/resources
- NILOA: www.learningoutcomeassessment.org/publications.html www.learningoutcomesassessment.org/ABstudentaffairs.htm www.learningoutcomeassessment.org/TFComponentAR.htm
- Texas A&M: assessment.tamu.edu/resources/Bibliography_ for_Assessment_2012-11-07.pdf
- Temple University: www.temple.edu/studentaffairs/assess ment/books.html
- The Ohio State University's Center for the Study of Student Life: Two websites: http://cssl.osu.edu/training-webinars/ or http://cssl.osu.edu/resources1

Create a Division Assessment Website

A division-specific assessment website has the benefit of being specific to the institution by providing staff members access to the dictionary of terms, the assessment handbook, commonly used templates, assessment examples from department programs, and professional publications and presentations by staff. Some great examples include, but are certainly not limited to, the following:

- Boston College: www.bc.edu/offices/vpsa/staffresources/Assess ment.html
- Indiana University-Purdue University Indianapolis: student affairs.iupui.edu/about/assessment
- Northern Illinois University: niu.edu/stuaff/planningassess ment/index.shtml
- Portland State University: www.pdx.edu/studentaffairs/assessment

- Texas A&M University: studentlifestudies.tamu.edu/
- The Ohio State University: cssl.osu.edu
- University at Albany: www.albany.edu/studentsuccess/assessment/
- University of Georgia: studentaffairs.uga.edu/assess/
- University of Houston: www.uh.edu/dsa/about_student_affairs/assessment_planning/index.html
- University of Memphis: saweb.memphis.edu/sala/
- University of Oregon: sa-assessment.uoregon.edu/

Use the Council for the Advancement of Standards in Higher Education

CAS (2015) offers standards for 44 functional areas in student affairs, each with an associated self-assessment guide to evaluate programs and services. There are professional standards for student services, academic support programs, and related programs and services. Staff members can use the standards to design programs and services to their institution-specific highest standards or to conduct self-assessment of their programs and services. CAS has also embedded student learning and development outcomes into the following six domains, each included in each functional area standard:

1. Knowledge acquisition, construction, integration, and application
2. Cognitive complexity
3. Intrapersonal development
4. Interpersonal competence
5. Humanitarianism and civic engagement
6. Practical competence

To obtain detailed information about the CAS standards and learning domains, visit their website (www.cas.edu/standards).

Promote Involvement in Professional Student Affairs Organizations

Involvement in professional organizations helps sharpen assessment skills and provides the added benefit of learning from colleagues who share similar work experiences, challenges, and issues. Just about every functional area of student affairs has a professional organization. Many assessment professionals find a professional home in the Association of Institutional Research (AIR), a leading national association in the field. AIR has numerous statewide chapters offering affordable opportunities to meet others in the local area, typically for a daylong annual conference. In addition, both ACPA and NASPA have strong communities of assessment practitioners who serve as members of the directorate board of a commission (ACPA) or knowledge community (NASPA) devoted to supporting assessment in student affairs. Finally, a newer organization, SAAL, is devoted specifically to those who work full-time in student affairs assessment, and it provides an invaluable community for sharing ideas and resources both online and through a vibrant electronic mailing list.

The tools and resources to build assessment competency are abundant, so one does not have to create teaching materials from scratch. As such, the assessment coordinator has both informal and formal opportunities to educate and coach student affairs colleagues as needed.

Assessment Trainings

While many think of training as something that occurs in a formalized setting, assessment coordinators often are helping others build their knowledge and skills in assessment in many different settings. Keeping a broad perspective on when/how training can occur helps to provide those educational moments that are needed in order to be successful.

Informal Assessment Training

Informal training occurs naturally by capturing those teachable moments with staff. Through these unplanned interactions, the assessment coordinator acts as consultant and facilitator, helping staff members feel more confident in their assessment knowledge and practice, working through projects together, and helping people "close the loop" to see the usefulness of data.

Formal Assessment Training

Formal assessment training is planned in advance. These trainings need to start first with the assessment team or a group of staff charged with (and/or who have an interest in) assessment practice. By building the skills of a small number of "assessment champions," the work of infusing assessment throughout the division becomes infinitely easier. At Portland State University, the Student Affairs Assessment Council was initially made up of 25 representative staff members from across the division who were selected because they were already doing some assessment in their departments and/or had expressed interest in doing assessment for their departments. It was essential to build the skill set of these members so that they could then champion assessment in their respective departments. The university built assessment competency through a series of seven integrated two-hour workshops that included developing an assessment plan and an assessment instrument.

Other formal trainings can occur through assessment boot camps and group workshops, at assessment conferences, and through assessment institutes. An assessment boot camp is a great way for an assessment coordinator to train an assessment committee on his or her campus. This usually happens during the summer, and it often involves leading staff members through a series of workshops from start to finish: research questions, data collection, data analysis, reporting, and using data for improvement. It can start off an academic year with a renewed energy around assessment.

In addition, some national conferences provide formal training in the context of working with professionals from other institutions. There are a number of assessment institutes and assessment conferences available nationwide. Assessment institutes typically offer more in-depth assessment training, often leading participants through all phases of the assessment process. The ACPA Student Affairs Assessment Institute serves as an opportunity for practitioners to learn about essential functions of assessment (data collection, analysis, reporting, using for improvement) in a supportive environment as a hands-on, intensive three-day experience. A powerful idea is to travel to such an institute with a team of practitioners who share a goal of developing a specific assessment program as a result of participating in the institute.

Assessment conferences, on the other hand, offer opportunities for sharing best practices and networking with colleagues from all over the country. The NASPA Assessment and Persistence Conference is an example of a national student affairs assessment conference, and there are numerous regional drive-in conferences based at specific institutions that serve a similar purpose (Texas A&M, Oregon, and Ohio State, to name just a few). Individuals or groups can travel to these opportunities to gain as much information as possible from other colleagues. Regardless of the choice of an institute or a conference, the assessment coordinator can help staff members think about which type of professional development for student affairs assessment would best move the division's efforts forward.

Other formalized instruction can occur through brown-bag or learn-at lunches, book readings, and webinars with facilitated discussions. Staff training can occur in a variety of ways: informal to formal and individual to group, so consider using a variety of methods to meet staff members where they are.

Sustaining Assessment Momentum

Once staff members are actively engaged in assessment, sustaining momentum is essential. Following are a few ideas to keep momentum:

- Encourage (and even expect) staff members to present internal assessment results to peers. This can occur through a variety of means, including presentations during unit and department meetings, assessment day(s), and brown-bag lunches.
- Reinforce collaborations in scholarship and expect members to publish and present assessment findings to both external and internal audiences.
- Reward and celebrate successes. Recognize progress made in assessment practice and hold annual assessment awards to acknowledge levels of competency in practice. For example, Portland State University recognizes emerging and exemplary in student affairs assessment practice annually at their spring division meeting.
- Partner in assessment. Building collaborations is essential and gets practitioners out of their department silos to see their impact on student learning on a large scale.

- Share assessment findings to increase transparency, to increase collaborations, and to limit assessment duplication.
- Invite external speakers to present to staff. With limited funds this may seem like an unlikely option, but speakers can be brought to campus virtually.
- Attend conferences with colleagues. If travel funds are limited, consider regional conferences.
- Hold an assessment day. Many campuses share and celebrate assessment either through a miniconference-type offering or post-sessions. Boston College, University of Michigan, University of Vermont, University at Buffalo, and Northern Arizona University all have these events; some have mentions on websites.

Lessons Learned/Overcoming Barriers to Assessment

- Provide practical, real-world examples and projects for staff members to work on to bring training to life. Make sure to encourage practice and skill development, too.
- Use an inquiry-based model to explore the burning questions staff members hold about their programs and series. These questions become the foundation for conducting assessment.
- Help staff members explore their "why"—why their programs and services exist. This will allow them to explore what occurs as a result of their programs and how it occurs for students.
- Begin with the end in mind in terms of impact on student learning. What are the end results of our efforts that we need to know work or don't work?
- Recognize assessment progress. Programs start at different places, so recognizing growth is important to keeping staff engaged in assessment. Meet staff members where they are and recognize progress in their growth, as well.
- Make assessment easier by starting with fewer outcomes to measure and using existing data as much as possible to measure these outcomes.
- Show staff members the power of getting out of their silos and working across student affairs and the campus. Encourage staff to share data and findings.

- Reinforce that assessment can be fun when we think of our programs and services as classrooms, where staff members are the teachers who get to explore what students feel, know, and can do.

In conclusion, one of the best ways to develop staff talent and capacity for assessment is to focus on telling the story of the cocurricular learning experience through collaboration across departments. The field of student affairs assessment must improve the way it tells this story in order to help decision makers understand key areas where students learn outside the classroom. In the classroom, faculty and administrators can track student learning via course assignments, student portfolios, and other aspects of the academic experience. However, outside the classroom, learning can be much less linear and therefore more difficult to measure. It is the responsibility of the student affairs profession to depict the out-of-class learning experience as a crucial component of the overall college academic experience. Therefore, for the cocurriculum to be understood by academic colleagues, the student affairs field must work to develop staff capacity for assessment so administrators can continually demonstrate where learning occurs outside the classroom and the impact of programs and services on student and institutional success.

References

American College Personnel Association. (2007). *Assessment skills and knowledge: Content standards for student affairs practitioners and scholars (ASK)*. Washington, DC: American College Personnel Association.

American College Personnel Association. (n.d.). *Professional competency areas for student affairs practitioners: Rubrics for professional development*. Retrieved from www.acpa.nche.edu/sites/default/files/professional-comp-rubrics.pdf

American College Personnel Association & National Association of Student Personnel Administrators Joint Task Force on Professional Competencies Standards. (2010). *Professional competency areas for student affairs practitioners*. Retrieved from www.naspa.org/images/uploads/main/Professional_Competencies.pdf

Bresciani, M. J., Gardner, M. M., & Hickmott, J. (2010). *Demonstrating student success: A practical guide to outcomes-based assessment of learning and development in student affairs*. Sterling, VA: Stylus.

Bresciani, M. J., Zelna, C. L., & Anderson, J. A. (2004). *Assessing student learning and development: A handbook for practitioners*. Washington, DC: National Association of Student Personnel Administrators.

Council for the Advancement of Standards in Higher Education. (2015). *CAS professional standards for higher education* (9th ed.). Washington, DC: Council for the Advancement of Standards in Higher Education.

Schuh, J. M., Upcraft, M. L., & Associates. (2001). *Assessment practice in student affairs: An applications manual.* San Francisco: Jossey-Bass.

Student Affairs Leadership Council. (2009). *The data-driven student affairs enterprise: Strategies and best practices for instilling a culture of accountability.* Washington, DC: Advisory Board Company.

Suskie, L. A. (2009). *Assessing student learning: A common sense guide* (2nd ed.). San Francisco: Jossey-Bass.

Yousey-Elsener, K. M. (2013). *Successful assessment in student affairs: A how-to guide.* Little Falls, NJ: PaperClip Communications.

7

Tenet Seven: Connecting Assessment to Planning, Decision Making, and Resource Allocation

James R. Doyle
Ellen S. Meents-DeCaigny

CREATING AN evidence-based culture requires intention and should start with leadership support and a thoughtful, integrated assessment model. In order to support organizational planning, decision making, and resource allocation, the culture should be established division-wide and structured to integrate data from across the organization. An integrated approach to assessment is a top-down and bottom-up initiative, meaning that everyone in the organization has a responsibility for the delivery of the initiative (Busby & Robinson, 2012). Another component of integration is consideration for how data collected in the organization—in this case, a division of student affairs—connect to other institutional data and what data the chief student affairs officer (CSAO) needs to be a well-informed institutional leader. The purpose of this chapter is to address how an integrated assessment model can help support organizational planning, decision making, and resource allocation.

Integrated Assessment Model

In order to link assessment to planning, decision making, and resource allocation, it is necessary to systematically collect consistent and varying types of data from across the division or organization. "A frequent mistake educators make is to pile up pieces of assessment without taking stock of the whole picture" (Walvoord, 2010, p. 32). Data related to the achievement of learning outcomes are important, but data related to the delivery of programs and services are also necessary to construct a complete picture of how the department and the division are achieving organizational goals, as well as contributing to overall institutional goals. Therefore, an integrated assessment model not only incorporates data from units across the division but also includes varying types of data in order to provide a more complete picture of organizational effectiveness. Collecting varying types of data across multiple units also allows for data to be compressed or dissected for multiple purposes, such as planning and decision making.

As one example, DePaul University's integrated assessment model (see Figure 7.1) is grounded in the mission of both the university and the division. Using the mission and goals of the division as a guide, the next steps are to develop divisional learning outcomes that define cocurricular learning across the division, and determine divisional success factors, which are data points that represent the impact and

Figure 7.1   DePaul University's integrated divisional assessment model.

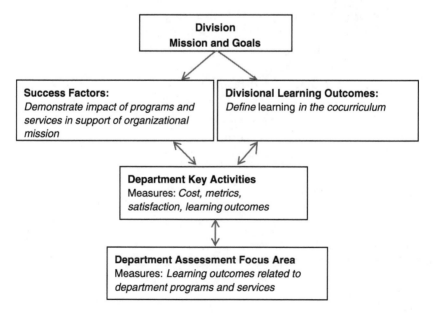

effectiveness of programs and services across the division. Success factors can include data related to the various types of programs and services provided, as well as metrics, such as the number of programs and the number of participants.

The work of the division is made up of the work being done in the departments, so the data needed to demonstrate achievement of divisional learning outcomes and the impact and effectiveness of programs and services must come from departments. Departments must take time to define *cocurricular learning* in their units and link department learning outcomes to divisional outcomes. Likewise, departments must also outline their key activities. *Key activities* are the programs and services a department is responsible for on a day-to-day basis and are used to measure department performance throughout the academic year. Key activities can be measured according to cost, metrics (e.g., number of programs, participants, partners, etc.), other assessment data (e.g., satisfaction data or impact data), and learning outcomes. Not all departments contribute to all divisional success factors or learning outcomes, but all department key activities are linked to a subset of divisional success factors and student learning outcomes to help demonstrate impact and effectiveness at the divisional level. For example, if there are seven divisional learning outcomes, all departments may argue they contribute to all seven in some way. However, in order to keep assessment focused and less overwhelming, each department should select three or four divisional outcomes to which they are primary contributors. For instance, university counseling services might focus on demonstrating learning related to intra- and interpersonal development, persistence and academic achievement, and intellectual skills and practical competence, and not focus on knowledge integration, faith development, leadership development, and intercultural maturity. Other departments, such as university ministry or student involvement and leadership would choose a different set of the seven divisional learning outcomes on which to focus.

In addition to collecting key activity data that measure the department's performance, each department conducts one or more annual assessment projects that focus on student learning related to department learning outcomes. In this model, because department outcomes are mapped to divisional learning outcomes, data collected at the department level can speak to divisional outcomes. By taking time to map learning outcomes from the bottom up—from the activity level, to the program level, to the department, to the division, and so on—any outcome assessed at a lower level (e.g., activity) can contribute to understanding learning at a higher level (e.g., department or divisional). Figure 7.1 illustrates this described integrated assessment model.

It is also important to consider how student affairs data are connected to and integrated with other data at the institution. An assessment coordinator may want to determine which institutional units are potential partners and what processes are in place for student affairs to either share or integrate data with these partners. Units responsible for institutional research, assessment in the colleges and schools, program review, and enrollment management are a few places to look for partners. Some examples of how data can be integrated include mapping divisional learning outcomes to institutional outcomes and sharing assessment results to demonstrate the division's contribution to student learning. Another way might be using retention and graduation data provided by institutional research to assess retention and graduation rates for student populations participating in divisional programs and services. Figure 7.2 illustrates possible ways data from student affairs can or should be connected to institutional data.

Figure 7.2   Integrating student affairs and institutional data.

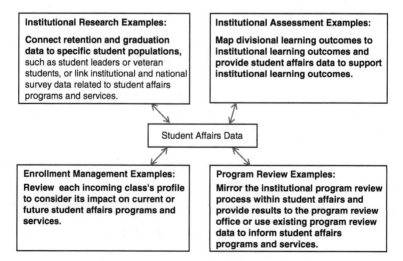

Institutional Research Examples:

Connect retention and graduation data to specific student populations, such as student leaders or veteran students, or link institutional and national survey data related to student affairs programs and services.

Institutional Assessment Examples:

Map divisional learning outcomes to institutional learning outcomes and provide student affairs data to support institutional learning outcomes.

Student Affairs Data

Enrollment Management Examples:
Review each incoming class's profile to consider its impact on current or future student affairs programs and services.

Program Review Examples:
Mirror the institutional program review process within student affairs and provide results to the program review office or use existing program review data to inform student affairs programs and services.

Assessment and Strategic Planning

Strategic planning and assessment go hand in hand. Assessment data can be used to help develop plans and measure achievement toward plan goals. According to Mittenthal (2002, pp. 2–9), the following are 10 keys to success for strategic planning:

1. A clear and comprehensive grasp of external opportunities and challenges
2. A realistic and comprehensive assessment of organizational strengths and limitations
3. An inclusive approach
4. An empowered planning committee
5. Involvement of senior leadership
6. Shared responsibility by board and staff members
7. Learning from best practices
8. Clear priorities and an implementation plan
9. Patience
10. A commitment to change

Of the 10 keys outlined, the first, second, and eighth are closely tied to assessment. Planning priorities and measuring progress and success will be difficult without a clear understanding of external opportunities and challenges, a realistic assessment of organizational strengths and limitations, and a clear implementation plan. Beyond using assessment to develop and implement a strategic plan, assessment can also be connected to planning in that specific strategic objectives can be incorporated into the plan to improve practices and increase staff capacity related to assessment.

Developing a Strategic Plan

When developing a strategic plan, it is important to assess what data (both external and internal to the organization) can help inform the planning process. As Mittenthal (2002) suggests, a clear understanding of external opportunities and challenges can offer guidance when determining key goals and objectives. Suggested places to look for external data include the institution's strategic plan, the institution's goals and outcomes, and the core curriculum. Institutional enrollment data and survey data can also be helpful. For example, institutional surveys of continuing and graduating students can provide insight into satisfaction with and usage of current programs and services, as well as awareness of the institution's mission. National surveys, such as the National Survey of Student Engagement (NSSE), can provide insight into how institutions provide resources and structure the curriculum and other learning opportunities to foster student engagement in activities that are linked to student learning (NSSE, 2014). Keep in mind, data on national trends can also give insight to what current issues or challenges face higher education and should be considered for planning purposes. For example, with the current focus on college completion, it would be helpful to monitor four-, five-, and six-year graduation rates.

After scanning the external environment for data to inform the planning process, it is important to look internally for data to understand the organization's strengths and limitations. When using an integrated assessment model, data collected across the division on an annual basis and throughout the year can be used to inform the process. For example, department key activities can provide insight into program impact, program costs, and student satisfaction with programs and services. Annual department assessment projects can provide data on the effectiveness of specific programs, and data related to divisional learning outcomes and success factors can provide a broader picture of data collected across departments. Other divisional data to consider are department self-studies, program reviews, and other survey data collected in the division.

Measuring Progress and Success

Being able to measure progress and achievement toward a strategic plan begins with clear goals, objectives, and activities. Because measuring progress most likely occurs at the activity level, clearly describing measurable milestones to achieve strategic activities is critical. Some activities are easier to measure, such as an increase in participant numbers related to a particular program, but other activities, such as the development and implementation of new programs and collaborations, may be more difficult to measure. One suggestion is to develop milestones for each activity and calculate each milestone as a percentage toward achievement of the activity. For example, if developing divisional student learning outcomes is a strategic activity and the process is broken down into five milestones, each milestone is assigned an equal percentage of achievement totaling 100% achievement of the goal. If the first two milestones include selecting divisional committee members (worth 20%) and reviewing well-established learning outcomes developed by the Association of American Colleges and Universities (AAC&U) and the Council for the Advancement of Standards in Higher Education (CAS) (worth 20%), then completion of these two steps would indicate 40% of the activity is achieved. Using this approach to track progress toward achievement of the plan requires thoughtful consideration of who is most qualified to develop milestones for an activity, since completion of milestones will be interpreted as achievement or success.

Assessment as a Strategic Goal

Developing assessment as a goal within a strategic plan offers an opportunity to focus on improving assessment within the division. Depending on where the division is in developing an assessment model, defining learning outcomes, determining department key activities, or building staff capacity related to assessment, assessment goals, and objectives can be incorporated into the plan to push the division to the next level. As mentioned in the previous section, strategic activities such as developing divisional learning outcomes can be incorporated into a plan, setting assessment as a priority for the division and allowing for a thoughtful approach to the process. And while CSAOs may wish assessment initiatives to be implemented swiftly, being strategic regarding how assessment activities are executed can reduce unrealistic expectations for staff and encourage more thoughtful and sustainable initiatives. Some intentional activities to consider writing into a strategic plan include reviewing current assessment processes, building staff capacity, developing or strengthening student learning outcomes, developing tools to manage data and information, and strengthening collaborations with institutional partners who also have responsibility for assessment and data management.

Assessment and Decision Making

It is through a comprehensive assessment initiative that institutional leaders can better understand how well they are meeting the organization's mission and goals and can make informed decisions about how to address gaps in organizational effectiveness. According to Schuh et al. (2009), "Questions of organizational effectiveness can be answered through a comprehensive assessment program" (p. 9), and leaders who do not have data to demonstrate mission and goal achievement or data to inform decisions are putting their organizations at risk. In regard to student affairs divisions, Schuh et al. (2009) stated:

> Without a systematic approach to gathering information and using that information to determine effectiveness of student affairs units, initiatives, programs and procedures, unit leaders will have difficulty determining whether organizational goals are being met, thus making their organizations vulnerable to reorganization, outsourcing, or even elimination. (p. 9)

Those responsible for developing a division-wide approach to assessment must consider what data are needed to enable university leadership, the CSAO, and departments within the division to make informed decisions. Knowing the needs of these three constituents helps determine what data to systematically collect at the department and divisional levels to inform decisions and address organizational effectiveness. For example, student demographic data related to student participation in a particular program can offer the department insight into whether it is reaching its target audience or reaching a broad enough audience according to program goals, the amount of personnel time dedicated to the program, and the overall cost. At the divisional level, student demographic data for this particular program can be combined with demographic data from other programs to see a bigger picture of student engagement across departments. Based on the data, the department and the division can make decisions as to whether programs are achieving intended goals.

As an institutional leader, it is important that the CSAO has data to not only demonstrate how the division is achieving its mission and goals and data to leverage when participating in institutional decision making, but also address important student issues. As a strong voice for important student issues on campus, the CSAO needs compelling evidence to be able to advocate on behalf of students. Data can help the CSAO and other important leaders understand how many students are impacted by a particular issue or if additional resources are needed to expand programs and services to address an issue. For example, when addressing the concern of student homelessness and food insecurities, it is important to track annually how many students report being homeless and having food insecurities and, if possible, to categorize types or levels of food insecurities. Based on the data, the CSAO can then make informed decisions about whether current services and personnel levels are sufficient to address the issue. Collecting various types of data to inform decisions is important. However, once a division has enough data and the right kinds of data, issues to consider are: How are the data informing decision making? What decisions are still being made without data that might be helpful (Walvoord, 2010)? Walvoord (2010) suggested spending time mapping how data flow into decision making. Although she focuses on mapping assessment data across the institution, the same principles can apply within student affairs. The mapping diagram Walvoord (2010) outlined includes the following three components:

1. **Data.** What are the various kinds of data you have about student learning?
2. **Digestion.** How are these data "digested"—that is, aggregated, analyzed, and disseminated?
3. **Decisions.** How are these data used for decisions, policies, planning, and budgeting (p. 32)?

Walvoord (2010) suggests, when constructing a diagram, that data are represented in boxes along the bottom, digestion in the middle, and decisions at the top (see Figure 7.3). Arrows are used to map connections from bottom to top between the three components. Any lack of arrows can indicate missing connections or opportunities. Walvoord's (2010) diagram highlights that knowing what evidence is needed to make decisions is important but stepping back to see how evidence is being used, or not used, to make decisions is also important.

Figure 7.3 Walvoord's ideal assessment system.

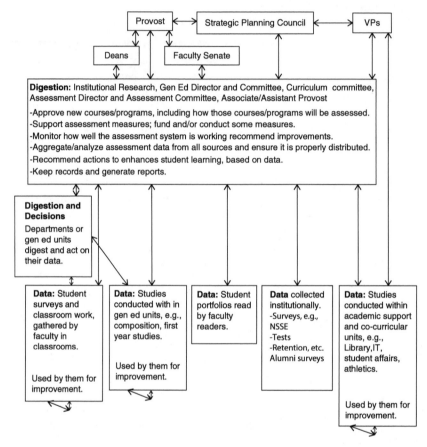

Note: Walvoord, B. E. (2010). *Assessment clear and simple: A practical guide to institutions, departments, and general education.* San Francisco, CA: Jossey-Bass. © 2010 John Wiley & Sons. Reprinted with kind permission.

Assessment and Resource Allocation

Assessment can inform many decisions that need to be made at the divisional level, but one particularly critical area is resource allocation. In 2001, Schuh et al. wrote: "Student affairs (was) under considerable pressure to demonstrate its importance and worth. In an era of declining resources and increased competition for what precious few resources there are, student affairs has come under the institutional financial microscope" (p. 9).

Thirteen years later, resources are still declining and student affairs divisions must continue to demonstrate good stewardship of how university resources are allocated and present strong evidence for any new resources requested. By establishing an evidence-based culture that is outcomes oriented and data driven, CSAOs and other student affairs professionals are better able to provide objective data to support funding requests (Culp, 2012).

One way to determine how divisional resources are to be allocated to support programs and services is to conduct an activity-mapping exercise. At DePaul University this exercise is facilitated by gathering pieces of evidence regarding department key activities, collected as part of the integrated assessment model (Figure 7.1), to help determine the effectiveness, overall impact, and potential overlap of programs and services. For example, if reviewing transition programs for first-year and transfer students housed in the Office of New Student and Family Engagement (NSFE), evidence such as program costs, participation numbers, student demographic data, number of programs facilitated, and number of personnel involved in the program would provide a snapshot of program reach versus program cost. Evidence regarding satisfaction data and learning outcomes assessment measured against program goals and outcomes could help speak to the level of effectiveness. Other questions to consider might be: Which departments collaborate with NSFE to facilitate transition programs? Are any departments duplicating services provided by NSFE? Ideally, this activity-mapping project would be conducted for all key activities within all departments at the same time so that a full picture of how resources are being allocated within and across the division could be considered.

Research by the Education Advisory Board (2009) suggested that student affairs divisions who were interested in effectively managing resources, particularly during cost-cutting periods, began by reviewing their current budget and then reflecting on future budgeting scenarios. "The starting point for this review is a formal process of cataloging all current efforts; this inventory provides an opportunity to identify redundancies and highlights opportunities for collaboration across the university" (Education Advisory Board, 2009, p. 12). The integrated assessment model proposed in Figure 7.1 can provide the pieces of evidence needed to facilitate a formal process of mapping or cataloging how resources are being used in order to

Figure 7.4   Humboldt State University prioritization pyramid.

Note: "Humboldt State University Prioritization Pyramid." From *Managing Through the Downturn: Strategies for Cost-Ccutting and Revenue Generation in Student Affairs Organizations.* Washington, DC: Education Advisory Board. © 2009 The Advisory Board Company. All rights reserved. Reprinted with permission.

determine where resources are needed and, perhaps, what programs and services need to be eliminated so resources can be redistributed.

The Education Advisory Board (2009) also discovered a prioritization process utilized by Humboldt State University to assess "how non-instructional programs and services contribute to institutional goals" (p. 21). Figure 7.4 illustrates the prioritization pyramid that was created for the process. For student affairs divisions, this pyramid can be used to evaluate specific programs and services, or it can be used at the department level. For example, if assessing prioritization of departments, the Center for Students With Disabilities would fall into level 1 because of required laws and the need to provide services for students with learning and physical disabilities in order for education to take place. A department such as counseling service may fall into level 2 since it is not required by law but necessary to support student success and academic achievement. On the other hand, depending on the institution's mission and goals, counseling services could also be placed in level 3 and considered a value-added

service that could be outsourced. The overall purpose of this prioritization process is to "facilitate institution-wide discussion about
mission critical areas and resource allocation" (Education Advisory
Board, 2009, p. 21).

Another way to demonstrate a need for resources to support the
academic mission and help the university meet its priorities is to
use workload data (Varlotta, 2012). According to Varlotta (2012),
"In student affairs, workload estimators can be used to reflect how
long it reasonably takes to complete a unique activity" (p. 113). For
example, how long does it take the dean of students to process an
academic withdrawal application? The estimated amount of time
spent on each withdrawal application would be multiplied by the
total number of withdrawal applications within a set period of time
(e.g., one semester). The resulting total indicates how many staff
hours are needed to support the academic withdrawal process, which
in turn helps determine how many staff members are needed to complete the activity in the allotted time. This process can be particularly
helpful for unique activities that are considered essential and require
a lot of staff time, such as advising or one-on-one interventions.

These are just a few examples of how a culture of evidence can
support divisional decisions related to resource allocation. Although
there are many other ways in which a division can use evidence to support resource allocation, the key is to have solid evidence and know
the organization's goals and priorities. According to Culp (2012), "A
culture of evidence leads to a more focused and fine-tuned institution and increases the accuracy and efficiency with which resources
are allocated" (p. 6).

Conclusion

Creating an evidence-based culture within a division requires a significant amount of staff commitment and time, but it is important
in order to support organizational planning, decision making, and
resource allocation. Such an initiative may take several years to fully
develop—to develop an integrated assessment model, implement
assessment processes, increase staff capacity related to assessment,
and collect useful data. The key to getting started is strong support
from the CSAO, an understanding of what data are needed for the

various constituencies, and how data will be used at varying levels of the organization.

References

Busby, K., & Robinson, B. G. (2012). Developing the leadership team to establish and maintain a culture of evidence in student affairs. In M. M. Culp & G. J. Dungy (Eds.), *Building a culture of evidence in student affairs: A guide for leaders and practitioners* (pp. 35–59). Washington, DC: NASPA Student Affairs Administrators in Higher Education.

Culp, M. M. (2012). Starting the culture of evidence journey. In M. M. Culp & G. J. Dungy (Eds.), *Building a culture of evidence in student affairs: A guide for leaders and practitioners* (pp. 1–19). Washington, DC: NASPA Student Affairs Administrators in Higher Education.

Education Advisory Board. (2009). *Managing through the downturn: Strategies for cost-cutting and revenue generation in student affairs organizations.* Washington, DC: Education Advisory Board.

Mittenthal, R. A. (2002). *Ten keys to successful strategic planning for nonprofit and foundation leaders.* Retrieved from www.tccgrp.com/pdfs/per_brief_tenkeys.pdf

National Survey of Student Engagement. (2014). *About NSSE.* Retrieved from nsse .iub.edu/html/about.cfm

Schuh, J. H. & Associates. (2009). *Assessment methods for student affairs.* San Francisco, CA: Jossey-Bass.

Varlotta, L. E. (2012). Designing and implementing a culture of evidence action plan. In M. M. Culp & G. J. Dungy (Eds.), *Building a culture of evidence in student affairs: A guide for leaders and practitioners* (pp. 103–119). Washington, DC: NASPA Student Affairs Administrators in Higher Education.

Walvoord, B. E. (2010). *Assessment clear and simple: A practical guide to institutions, departments, and general education.* San Francisco, CA: Jossey-Bass.

8

Tenet Eight: Cultivating Ethical Assessment Practice

Kimberly Yousey-Elsener
Becki Elkins

ONE OF the most far-reaching responsibilities of an assessment coordinator is being the primary adviser for the ethical use of data. This role touches on just about every action taken by an assessment coordinator and should be considered one of the primary responsibilities of anyone in the position. This role requires two competencies:

1. Knowing and applying ethical standards as they relate to research, assessment, data security, and the professional context in which we work
2. Guiding others to ensure that ethical standards are being followed in assessment work throughout the division

Knowing and Applying Ethical Standards

Ethics can be defined as "distinguishing right from wrong or substituting appropriate actions for inappropriate ones" (Timm & Lloyd, 2012, p. 54). In relation to assessment, ethics touches on issues such as protecting the rights of the people providing data or participating in studies; access and use of data; the sharing of data and information; data analysis; technology implementation; and maintaining the integrity of the data in a highly politicized environment. First and foremost, an assessment coordinator must be familiar with applicable ethical standards. According to the NASPA *Assessment Education Framework* (Student Affairs Administrators in Higher Education, 2009):

> Good assessment procedures must take into consideration how peo-
> ple will be impacted. The history of using human subjects in social
> science research includes many cases where people were "taken
> advantage of" and in many cases harmed. Federal law requires cer-
> tain procedures be followed to inform subjects of the potential for
> harm, while best practices prescribe methods for planning, execut-
> ing, analyzing and reporting findings. (p. 2)

Although many assessment coordinators have had some training in ethics, either through a formal graduate education program
or through human subjects training, reviewing various standards to
ensure that they can be applied in any pertinent situation is recommended to professionals starting a formal assessment role. In the
past this often required just going through data ethics training, but
in today's legal environment it is good practice to be familiar with
the following:

- Research ethics as determined through institutional review
  boards and human subjects procedures
- Federal laws related to the Family Educational Rights and
  Privacy Act (FERPA; www2.ed.gov/policy/gen/guid/fpco/
  ferpa/index.html) and the Health Insurance Portability and
  Accountability Act (HIPAA; www.hhs.gov/ocr/privacy)
- Ethical standards and principles determined by professional
  associations in any given area
- Institutional policies on data security, data sharing, and data
  access

Sources of information for each of these may vary by institution
or discipline but most information also has some common elements
that making applying various standards in day-to-day interactions a
little easier.

Research and Assessment Ethics

Depending on the size and scope of an institution, there may or may
not be an institutional review board (IRB), human subjects committee,

and/or ethics board to educate people about research ethics as well as provide guidance and approval for projects. Most of the assessment work performed in student affairs falls under "social science" research and is often considered "exempt" by these review boards. Regardless of whether the project is exempt or not, if the IRB, human subjects committee, or ethics committee on your campus offer training materials, online modules, or courses, it is highly recommended that at least one person from the division attend these trainings. A good first step is to check institution-specific policies and procedures to determine what is required and when. Although the formal process may not be required for an assessment project, the training provides information that should be applied to any attempt to collect, analyze, and report data.

When applying these concepts specifically to student affairs assessment, two resources offer strong guidance, case studies, and areas for consideration: "Ethical Assessment" written by Timm and Lloyd as part of ACPA's *Assessment in Practice: A Companion Guide to the ASK Standards* (2012) and "Ethics" written by Schuh et al. as part of their *Assessment Methods for Student Affairs* (2009) publication. Both chapters defined *ethical practice* using the model created by Kitchner (1985), which focused on five aspects:

1. Respect autonomy. Ensure that those participating in the assessment work are doing so voluntarily. This can be a challenge in an era where response rates are low, card-swiping and other technology makes it easier to track things without student knowledge, and yet the need for strong data is growing.
2. Do no harm. Ensure that those participating will not experience any negative impacts as a result of the data being collected. This can be as simple as ensuring that identifying information is not reported with specific assessment findings, providing counseling and other support resources when collecting data around high-risk topics, or making sure that whatever incentives being offered help support student success.
3. Benefit others. All data collecting should be done with the intention of increasing knowledge, awareness, or improvement. Collecting data to punish specific people or programs should be avoided. Likewise collecting data that are never intended to be used or shared should be avoided.

4. Be just. This includes fair treatment of all participants, making sure resources are shared appropriately, and providing equal access for participants as well as to final results. This item is especially important to consider when assessment practices need to be inclusive of diverse student populations. Students with accessibility needs, language barriers, race, ethnicity, religious, gender, or sexual orientation concerns should all be considered.
5. Be faithful. Staying true to the original purpose of the projects, using results in good faith to make changes, and being truthful in sharing data are all important aspects of assessment ethics.

This framework helps guide decisions about how data are collected, analyzed, and used on a campus. Learning more about specific IRB procedures provides more in-depth knowledge in these areas and helps apply these standards to everyday practice. If no IRB, human subjects, or ethics training is available on a specific campus, there are several online tutorials and videos that have been produced by other campuses that can be utilized instead. A simple Internet search provides many different sources. As an example, a series of videos can be found at Education Portal (education-portal .com/academy/topic/principles-of-ethical-research.html).

Federal Laws

Most of our work in student affairs is guided by one of two federal laws: FERPA and HIPPA (see p. 120). Both focus on data privacy and security related to students' academic and health records. Knowledge of these guidelines should shape conversations on what data can be collected and shared specifically related to areas such as grades, judicial records, counseling files, health service records, and other official student records. Whereas most assessment projects center on sharing aggregate data (or summary data that combine multiple students' information), care must be taken to ensure that data are being collected, accessed, stored, and shared in a manner consistent with these policies. If it is unclear how to follow these federal guidelines, there are usually professional staff members on campus that specialize in compliance with federal guidelines. They can often be found in health services, registrar's offices, legal services, and counseling centers.

Ethical Standards and Principles by National Associations

Depending on the project and department/unit, the people involved may be guided by one or more standards of ethical practice determined by a national association or organization. These standards can vary depending on the type of organization and its focus, but most have some common elements. It is also important to note that most of these standards are written from a larger framework that includes ethics beyond assessment and research but most include data collection and use, either explicitly or implicitly. A few to consider are the following:

- ACHA "General Statement of Ethical Principles and Guidelines" (Student Health and Wellness) (www.acha.org/publications/docs/ACHA_General_Statement_Ethical_Princi ples_May2010.pdf)
- ACPA's "Ethical Principles and Standards" (www.myacpa.org/sites/default/files/Ethical_Principles_Standards.pdf)
- "ACUHO-I Standards and Ethical Principles" (Residence Life and Housing) (www.acuho-i.org/Portals/0/2014_Feb_Stand ards_Ethical_Principles_1.pdf)
- American Psychology Association's (APA) "Ethical Principles of Psychologists and Code of Conduct" (www.apa.org/ethics/code/index.aspx)
- Council for the Advancement of Standards (CAS) (2012) "Statement of Shared Ethical Principles" (www.cas.edu/ethics)
- NASPA/ACPA Joint Competencies in Student Affairs Ethical Professional Practice (www.naspa.org/about/student-affairs/ethical-professional-practice)
- "NIRSA Professional Member Code of Ethics" (Campus Recreation) (www.nirsa.org/docs/About%20Us/Governing/Code_Of_Ethics-Pro.pdf)

- NODA "Statements of Ethical Standards" (Orientation, Transition, and Retention) (www.nodaweb.org/?page=ethical_stand ards)

Institutional Policies on Data Collection, Security, and Sharing

As technology becomes more pervasive, the amount of data stored in information technology (IT) systems increases. These systems allow for the possibility of more data being utilized by institutions for assessment purposes. Before implementing new technology or exchanging data between and across systems, consult with IT departments and perhaps legal services to determine the ramifications of sharing data. More campuses are creating policies and guidelines around using and sharing data, determining data "ownership" standards for data security when working with third-party vendors or between platforms and other considerations. Although many assessment coordinators have some technology expertise, it is wise to consult the data security experts for guidance in issues that involve exchanging large amounts of data between technology systems.

Guiding Others in Ethical Considerations

Assessment coordinators are usually responsible for not only being knowledgeable about guidelines and practices but also educating others. This guidance is done in both formal and informal settings, whether through workshops, assessment planning processes, policymaking, technology implementation, or everyday interactions where decisions need to be made about how data will be collected and used.

Linda Suskie (2009) suggested the following for using assessment results fairly, ethically, and responsibly:

- Make assessments planned and purposeful.
- Focus assessments on important . . . goals.

- Actively involve those with a stake in decisions stemming from the results.
- Communicate assessment information widely and transparently.
- Discourage others from making inappropriate interpretations or otherwise false or misleading statements about assessment results.
- Don't hold people accountable for things they cannot do (e.g., unrealistic timelines, data analysis that is too complicated, meeting unrealistic assessment targets).
- Don't penalize faculty and staff members whose assessment results are less than positive.
- Don't let assessment results dictate decisions.
- Promote the use of multiple sources of information when making major decisions.
- Keep faculty, students, and staff informed on how assessment findings support major decisions. (p. 299)

These generic guidelines can be applied along with IRB/ethics committee standards, FERPA/HIPAA regulations, and campus-specific policies. With all these resources available, it is often the role of the assessment coordinator to use them to help shape conversations and/ or bring up the appropriate guidelines to educate others when decisions are being made. Assessment coordinators often find this work being done in situations where they have a "teachable moment" such as the following:

- Assessment planning and consultation meetings
- Committee meetings
- One-on-one conversations
- Retreats
- Workshops

For example, an assessment coordinator is invited to the first-year planning committee meeting where members are talking about their assessment plan. The committee decides that response rates for their orientation evaluation survey have been low for the past few years. They have worked into the schedule that at the end of each day students are required to sit in a lecture hall and complete a paper survey. Students will not be able to leave until they have completed the survey. As the assessment coordinator, this is a great opportunity to bring up ethical considerations such as whether this might be considered coercing or forcing students to take the survey against their will. If students perceive they are being forced to take the survey, how will this affect results? Are there other techniques that could be used to increase response rates that might result in better data and more ethical procedures?

In addition to those teachable moments, there are also situations where the assessment coordinator makes a judgment call about data ethics. These can include the following:

- Data requests made by researchers and external/internal institutional affiliates for access to student data
- Technology implementation—keeping in mind that with increased technology comes the increased ability to access/share data and setting up systems with access rules and other protocols is important
- Decisions around what data or results to share with which audiences
- What to do with less positive or less favorable assessment results
- Decisions around what data analysis is appropriate given the data collected
- Policy creation
- Political situations where there is pressure to share or collect data inappropriately

For example, a faculty researcher affiliated with the university is seeking student e-mail addresses, GPA, and other demographic information to carry out a federally funded research grant. He has made a formal request for information via the dean of students' office (as per the institution's data policy); however, the research project has not been approved or exempted by the IRB. Further, the amount of data being requested violates institutional policy on student data requests and calls into question the need to share FERPA-protected student information in a secure manner. The assessment coordinator is asked by the dean's office to determine the best course of action.

When making these judgment calls, it is necessary to have a clear and transparent rationale behind the decision. When appropriate, consult with the direct supervisor. When in doubt, consult with an additional resource on campus to gain insight. Schuh et al. (2009) suggested the following resources: faculty member, IRB/ethics committee member, legal counsel, judicial affairs, office of human resources, registrar office, IT or data security office, and/or peers and colleagues in assessment and institutional research.

Whether it is a teachable moment or a judgment call, assessment coordinators have a responsibility to balance ethical guidelines, policies, and procedures with the need to gather useful data and sometimes competing priorities related to that data. This can be a daunting task. A strong foundation in data ethics and readiness to apply this knowledge are essential parts of the assessment coordinator role. As with many things, when situations are complex it is often helpful to seek the guidance and consultation of others. The following case studies are designed to present some common scenarios and provide helpful conversations around carrying out this role.

Case Scenarios

When presented with a situation that requires a decision or action, Stage and Dannells (2000) suggested eight steps to analyze case scenarios:

1. Identify the decision issues present.
2. Determine the important facts in the case.
3. Identify additional information that needs to be gathered.
4. Identify the key actors in the case.
5. Determine relevant theories to be applied.
6. Identify potential alternative solutions.
7. Map out the advantages and disadvantages for each alternative.
8. Select a reasonable course of action.

The following case studies highlight situations that assessment coordinators might encounter. In each scenario, imagine that you are the student affairs assessment coordinator and use the steps suggested by Dannells and Stage as well as assessment ethics to determine a course of action for responding.

Focus Groups and Confidential Data

Two hall directors and an area coordinator in residence life have proposed an assessment project examining substance abuse in the residence halls. They have met with you to discuss interest in using focus groups to gain a more realistic picture of the types of student substance use and abuse. When the assistant director of residence life is informed of the study, she asks to have the results shared directly with her and reminds the hall directors of their obligation to "write up" offenders. She indicates to the area coordinator that the information gleaned from the study should be used to "catch" students using drugs in the halls.

As student affairs assessment coordinator, some things to consider are the following:

- Confidentiality of focus group data
- Conflicts of interest related to selection of focus group facilitators and those involved in data analysis
- Political and power dynamics between supervisors and those who report to them when it comes to use of data

Reflection Questions:

- Can data collected for assessment be used for personal identification in judicial cases?
- Do situations exist where reporting what a student shares in a focus group could be appropriate? If so, what are the standards for making such a decision? Does this case meet those standards?
- What resources on your campus are available to staff members faced with supervisors who insist on using data inappropriately?
- What are some alternatives that can be proposed in this situation?

Surveys and Incentives

The Midwestern Community College Assessment Committee would like to administer a national survey on student engagement in the spring. The committee members are enthusiastic about the strategy they have developed for encouraging survey response. The incentive they have suggested is to allow students who complete the survey to participate in a drawing for first place in the coming year's room selection process.

Items to consider include the following:

- Appropriate strategies for encouraging study participation
- Fairness to both those who participate and those who opt out

Reflection Questions:

- What are the problems associated with giving students who complete the survey the opportunity to participate in the drawing for first place in room selection?
- What guidelines are in place on your campus to ensure fairness in encouraging study participation? What additional guidelines should be considered or reviewed?
- How can you help redirect the committee's enthusiasm?
- Are there alternatives that can be proposed in this situation?

Data Requests

The student activities office at East Coast College coordinates Family Weekend. The new director has submitted a request for a list of all students, their IDs, and phone numbers as well as their parents' names, addresses, and phone numbers. When you ask about the request, the director informs you that he intends to do a follow-up survey of Family Weekend similar to the one he administered at his previous institution. He plans to start with a written survey and then have his staff members call students and their parents to ask about their experiences.

Items to consider include the following:

- FERPA guidelines, in general and specific to your campus

- Giving out contact information to surveyors versus sending out surveys for them
- Possible conflicts of interest with other offices contacting parents

Reflection Questions:

- What are your campus's specific policy guidelines pertaining to FERPA?
- What does your campus policy consider "directory" (i.e., public) information?
- What alternatives might you suggest to the director? How might you help him while maintaining privacy expectations?

Assessment and Performance Evaluations

Each year, Western University's career center offers résumé-writing and career development workshops to the student body. At the end of each session, participants are asked to assess what they learned. The career center director asks you to generate a report for each career center staff member. She informs you that she is looking at the evaluations of the programs her staff members have presented and would like to look at their individual results compared to the results of rest of the staff. After some discussion, she acknowledges that she intends to use these reports as performance evaluations for each staff member.

Items to consider are the following:

- The potential for data to be used to "punish" or to "praise" people
- The power dynamics involved
- Potential detrimental effects of using assessment data for performance evaluations

Reflection Questions:

- What are the risks to the staff of using assessment data in this manner? Are the risks equally distributed across the staff?

- How might you redirect the director?
- What alternatives might you suggest?

These situations raise a myriad of issues and touch on all of Kitchner's (1985) ethical dimensions. They are not, however, atypical encounters for student affairs assessment professionals, furthering the importance of being well versed in student affairs and assessment ethics. Equipped with knowledge of Kitchner's principles as well as federal laws, institutional policies, and association ethical standards, student affairs assessment professionals have the capacity to ensure assessment is conducted ethically and with care for students and staff.

Conclusion

An assessment coordinator's role in cultivating ethical practice related to data collection is ongoing and will develop over time. Just as organizations continue to evolve, so too will the ethical situations that arise. As other factors, such as politics, are considered in the data collection equation, so too are ethics. This chapter is meant to be an introduction to some of the basic concepts around ethics and point the reader toward resources on most campuses that can be helpful in the conversation. As a new assessment coordinator, a good place to start is to check institution-specific policies and procedures, especially as they relate to human subjects, IRB, or ethics, as well as FERPA and HIPAA. Brush up on any training in these areas. Finally, use the issues presented in the case studies to take time to reflect on past situations and how these situations were resolved or as a way to anticipate your response to future issues that may arise.

References

Kitchner, K. S. (1985). Ethical principles and ethical decisions in student affairs. In H. J. Canon & R. D. Brown (Eds.), *Applied ethics in student affairs* (pp. 17–29). San Francisco, CA: Jossey-Bass.

Schuh, J. H., & Associates. (2009). *Assessment methods for student affairs*. San Francisco, CA: Jossey-Bass.

Stage, F. K., & Dannells, M. (2000). *Linking theory to practice: Case studies for working with college students*. New York, NY: Routledge.

Student Affairs Administrators in Higher Education. (2009). *Assessment education framework*. Retrieved fromwww.northwestern.edu/studentaffairs/assessment/media/pdfs/FrameworkBrochure-Dec09.pdf

Suskie, L. (2009). *Assessing student learning: A common sense guide*. San Francisco, CA: Jossey-Bass.

Timm, D. M., & Lloyd, J. (2012). Ethical assessment. In D. M. Timm, J. Davis Barham, K. McKinney, & A. Knerr (Eds.), *Assessment in practice: A companion guide to the ASK standards* (pp. 54–62). Washington, DC: ACPA.

9 Tenet Nine: Navigating Politics

Darby Roberts

PREVIOUS CHAPTERS have addressed the capacity-building role of the assessment coordinator. That person has to create a culture of assessment, provide professional development, share knowledge, sustain partnerships, and be an expert in assessment functions. In addition, that person must maintain high ethical standards in a dynamic environment. An assessment coordinator is in a role that transcends and influences departments, functions, and hierarchies. Clearly, student affairs assessment professionals do not operate in a vacuum. Individuals and their unique personalities combine into groups and, in turn, become organizations. Every group, no matter its purpose, inevitably faces conflict and disagreement about directions, resources, and strategies.

No matter the location and the people, politics are involved in the day-to-day workings as decisions are made. Because of that environment, assessment coordinators need to be keenly aware of the context in which they operate. Cavins-Tull (2012) described the development of the assessment specialist as a response to lack of skills among professionals and "political resistance" to the assessment process (p. 138). As a result, "Organizational leaders must persuade members to envision the value and benefits of assessment and create opportunities for unit or program leaders to be recognized for participating in evaluation" (p. 138). In this role, assessment coordinators must understand who makes decisions when, who controls the resources and directions, and who has positional and nonpositional power. An assessment coordinator works best by working with others to get things done with support from organizational leaders.

Upcraft and Schuh (2002) stated that assessment "virtually always occurs in a political context that the investigators must take into account in designing the assessment" (p. 19). Lis Dean (2013) provided guidance about politics in assessment, recognizing that whenever interests, resources, and people interact, politics exist. Within any group of people, there are a variety of perspectives, priorities, and interests. When these interests conflict, people behave in a political manner to get their goals accomplished.

Stakeholders with different, and sometimes competing, priorities complicate the decision-making process. The leadership of the institution, division, and department set priorities. Many institutions are facing scarce resources and are competing to gain more resources. Decisions about program funding can be based on assessment results (or lack thereof). Accrediting agencies are asking for more assessment data, especially regarding student learning and use of assessment results for change. Legislators may decrease funding based on their own political pressure regarding competing fund requests, voter pressure, and new policies for funding decisions. As Schuh and Upcraft (2000) noted, "Perhaps the most compelling reason that assessment findings often end up gathering dust on some policymaker's shelf is that the investigators fail to take into account the institutional *political* context" (p. 15).

Power is inherent in politics. Individuals and groups use power to advance their agendas and resolve conflicts. Positional power, identifying who is at the top of the chain of command, is fairly obvious, but there are also other forms of power (Lis Dean, 2013). People in positional power have control over resources, policies, and decision making based on their level in the hierarchical structure. On the other hand, people with expert power have a skill or knowledge in a certain area. For example, this could include faculty members or those with unique experiences or training. Referent power is built on personal relationships, rather than structural expectations. Finally, people with information power have or control access to data or knowledge that others need or want. For the assessment coordinator to be successful, he or she must understand who has what type of power and be aware of his or her own power in various situations and how that works in the larger organization. Depending on where the position is in the hierarchy, the assessment coordinator may or may not have positional power but will have information and expert power, and may develop referent power over time. Because people and environments change, assessment coordinators must continually pay attention to the power and politics.

A key part of the political process and power revolves around information. As an external consultant, the assessment coordinator has the ability to create, share, and hide information. For some staff members, assessment can be very scary because of the potential to share unflattering information. Because not all student affairs professionals have a passion for, or even an interest in assessment, the assessment coordinator uses specialized knowledge about data collection, analysis, and sharing to distribute information to various stakeholders. The assessment coordinator, in working with technology, data analysis, or even institutional researchers, has a skill and speaks a language unfamiliar to most others. In synthesizing various pieces of information, the assessment coordinator can impact who gets what information and the subsequent decisions in how information is used.

To illustrate these concepts in a student affairs context, the remainder of the chapter will focus on the six areas identified in *Assessment Skills and Knowledge: Content Standards for Student Affairs Practitioners and Scholars (ASK Standards)* (American College Personnel Association, 2006) related to the politics of assessment. The *ASK Standards* provided foundational language and content to guide all student affairs professionals, not just those in an assessment role. A follow-up publication, *Assessment in Practice: A Companion Guide to the ASK Standards* (Timm, Barham, McKinney & Knerr, 2013) provided more context and examples of most of the areas addressed in the *ASK Standards*. Following the explanation of each standard, a brief case study illustrates the political risks associated with that standard.

Standard A: Ability to Determine Political Risks That May Apply to Assessment Results and the Audiences Likely to Be Adversely Affected by Findings

Understanding how those with power will respond to the results is important. Assessment professionals have to think of how to effectively share "bad" or uncomfortable results before actually collecting data. This approach places the focus on using results for planning and improvement, rather than just gathering the results themselves. Assessment can have fiscal repercussions if the results indicate a program is not successful, especially in times of scarce resources. The assessment coordinator is probably just the messenger, rather than the program coordinator, and the programmatic reputational risk can be a scary endeavor for some units. Student affairs staff may have previously based their success on anecdotal evidence that their programs are beneficial. The assessment coordinator challenges staff members to provide more direct evidence, which may conflict with the anecdotes.

Staff members can also have an emotional reaction and fear the process and results. Fear is one of the biggest barriers to developing an assessment culture. The politically astute assessment coordinator can allay those fears by developing relationships, encouraging staff to start with a win, and ensuring that staff members are not personally evaluated based on assessment results.

Student affairs assessment professionals must have a broad view and understanding of who is impacted by assessment results. As identified in previous chapters, the stakeholders vary greatly and can include students (and their own subpopulations), staff, administration, faculty, parents, legislators, alumni, and more. Results that increase resources for one group may decrease resources for another. For example, conducting a campus climate study on underrepresented groups or sexual assault can illuminate disparities in treatment and perceptions of subpopulations. Those experiences may be affecting retention and graduation rates, which are a priority to most institutions. The institution may devote scarce resources to addressing the issues, which can take away from other priorities. On the other hand, if the institution does nothing after the results are published, the groups will once again feel marginalized. The media or other stakeholders can latch on to specific results, either positive or negative, which may alter the priorities of implementing change.

Because assessment coordinators work with a variety of stakeholders, sometimes with competing goals, it is important to collaborate with project sponsors throughout the process. Early in the process, the assessment coordinator and the sponsor should agree on the purpose, requirements, timeline, and reporting needs. In addition, they must agree on the confidentiality of the data and respondents. For example, staff members may want to hide data that do not reflect well on their programs or services. At the same time, assessment coordinators are proponents of sharing information so that improvements can be instituted and aim to provide a level of responsible transparency. When those differing perspectives conflict, it can become an uncomfortable situation. Defining these parameters early helps avoid political and ethical dilemmas that could explode at the end of the project. Expectations about sharing and using results should be communicated early and clarified often. Discussing the possibility of negative results before the data are collected and analyzed eliminates the surprise factor.

What would you do? You were asked to conduct a sexual assault campus climate survey. The results indicate students are unaware of the policies and resources, report incidences in greater number than those actually reported to the university, and are uncomfortable reporting. The institution's Title IX coordinator (not in your division) has been at the institution for a long time and does not want "bad press" on the issue.

Items to consider include the following:

- Organizational structure and context, especially who has what type of power
- Identifying where results are reported and to what audiences

Reflection Questions:

- What are the legal obligations to report and/or act on results?
- How might survey results be discussed without connecting them to job performance?
- Are there other champions for this issue on campus who could carry messages or take action?

Standard B: Ability to Use Assessment in the Context of Strategic Planning and Institutional Decision Making, Including the Use of Assessment to Effect Change When Warranted

Using assessment in planning and decision making may be a shift in philosophy at some institutions. It may even require organizations to work together in new ways to provide services and programs. "The demand for increased collaboration and for sharing information and resources will place new demands on student affairs organizations that have been traditionally siloed and vertically oriented in the way they interact within the institution" (Kuk, 2012a, p. 6). For example, many institutions are concerned with student retention and graduation, metrics which transcend any one particular program. In student affairs, departments must be able to articulate their contribution to student success more than they have in the past. The challenge is that "change in these organizations can be very difficult when either individuals or groups within the organization feel threatened by what is different" (Cavins-Tull, 2012, p. 134). With some effort, "organizations are seeing the value of and need for shared decision-making, more transparent and lateral communication, and more flexible and collaborative operational processes" (Kuk, 2012b, p. 18). Assessment can actually provide the framework for increased collaboration.

Ideally, assessment should be integrated with planning and budgeting. In reality, this is not always the case. If the institution requires a 10% cut in budget across the board in departments, and specific programs may need to be cut to meet this initiative, assessment should be able to contribute to the decision. Alternatively, maybe there is a windfall and extra money is available. What is the best use of the funding? Expanding a successful program, making changes to a struggling program to make it viable, or a combination of options? Even in stable years, assessment results should be incorporated into the planning and budgeting process. More vice presidents of student affairs rely on department assessment data and reports when planning and approving an overall division budget. Assessment in the department or division can guide where resources (human, fiscal, physical) are assigned.

Assessment coordinators should be looking for opportunities for collaboration, which could be in data collection or in analyzing results. For example, the health center participates in a national survey about student health behaviors. Staff members from the health center, the counseling center, and the recreation center could brainstorm about what the data say and how they could all work together to improve the mental and physical health of students. From a process perspective, the assessment coordinator may create a framework for the assessment process that focuses on how assessment informs planning. In an individual assessment project, the assessment coordinator could ask clients how they will use assessment results in planning and decision making. On a larger scale, there may be a framework to provide information to the vice president about how assessment results informed budgeting, planning, and program improvement.

What would you do? The division of student affairs operates in a decentralized and siloed manner. The most recent division strategic plan expired five years ago, and most departments do not have a current strategic or assessment plan. When a new vice president of student affairs is hired, she wants to see how each department has accomplished their own mission, as well as supported the division and university missions.

Items to consider include the following:

- The context around leadership change and how that is being perceived by units
- Current culture of assessment and how this request might serve to move it forward or establish a barrier

Reflection Questions:

- What evidence does each unit have that might serve this purpose?
- What is the history of sharing assessment data with leadership?
- How can expectations be clarified in order to provide useful information?

Standard C: Ability to Identify the Context/Institutional Factors That Shape the Need for the Assessment

Every institution has a different context—public/private, two year/four year, state/federal government influence, town/gown relationships, ratings, employer expectations, leadership changes versus stability, institution mission, student demographics, accreditation requirements, placement of student affairs in the institutions, and so on. Some institutions may be very focused on student retention and graduation, whereas others may be more concerned with garnering more research funding or developing online programs for nontraditional students.

Assessment coordinators may or may not report directly to the senior student affairs officer (SSAO) or other leadership position, but they may be asked to provide information to a person who can impact others. For example, Carreon (2011) stated that SSAOs should review the following information on a regular basis: internal data about makeup and functioning of the institution, data describing how the division functions are perceived by the larger college community, and data "related to demographic, technology, workforce, workplace, and economic trends and shifts" (p. 149). For student affairs divisions, the context may involve demonstrating how student affairs contributes to the institutional vision, mission, and values. In particular, student affairs organizations may be under further pressure to provide evidence of their contribution to student learning, retention, and graduation. In addition, student affairs must be able to articulate how it uses resources in an efficient and effective manner to support the larger organization. Particular issues, such as campus climate, sexual assault, and mental health may be seen as assessment topics owned by student affairs. These questions may arise more frequently in a highly politicized environment.

Whatever the context, the assessment coordinator has to understand the impact of the environment on the assessment agenda. Because higher education and institutions are dynamic, priorities may change when leadership changes, institutions face fiscal challenges, and so on. As Upcraft and Schuh (2002) stated, "Assessment needs might change drastically as a result of new leadership that requires different evidence of effectiveness, sees new problems, or devalues old problems" (pp. 18–19). Assessment coordinators need to be knowledgeable about general higher education topics (e.g., student persistence, the cost of higher education, diversity, and student learning); they must also know how those play out at specific institutions.

What would you do? The institution is planning to hire a newly created position, vice president for diversity and inclusion. The division of student affairs recently completed a campus climate survey that indicated most students were generally satisfied with the environment, although there were several areas identified that needed addressing. The provost told the vice president of student affairs to not release the much awaited report because it would interfere with the hiring of the vice president of diversity and inclusion.

Items to consider include the following:

- Organizational structure and context, especially who has what type of power
- Identifying where results are reported and to what audiences

Reflection Questions:

- What are the legal obligations to report and/or act on results?
- Is it possible to share assessment results privately in order to start taking action? Could the assessment data be used as part of the interview process?
- Are there other champions for this issue on campus who could carry messages or take action with a public sharing of data?
- Would a delay in reporting results have a large effect on the issues/needs being voiced by students?

Standard D: Ability to Report Assessment Findings With an Awareness of the Political Context for Those Results Such as Who Receives the Results, the Format in Which the Results Should Be Reported, and Timing of the Reporting

As a part of the assessment cycle, the assessment coordinator needs to pay close attention to how and when results are communicated. As Bresciani (2012) stated, "The importance of our ability to translate our research- and outcomes-based assessment results into terminology that those outside the profession can understand grows increasingly more every day" (p. 118). Multiple audiences, with different priorities and knowledge, may be interested in the results.

Bresciani (2012) also provided a reflective question to provide guidance to the assessment coordinator and department or division leadership:

> How do you provide information on the theories that inform your practice, the outcomes of your practice, the results from your assessment, and the resulting decisions to all members of the public so they will better understand what you do and want to partner with you in promoting students' success? (p. 120)

It is not only what you say but also how and when you say it that can have a political impact on the organization. Depending on the context of the institution, staff members need to understand open records laws of the state to know what, how, and under what circumstances data will be released to the public.

As a part of the planning process, the assessment coordinator needs to know the purpose, the intended audience, and the potential actions to be taken based on the information even before the data are collected. In addition, the assessment coordinator needs to be well versed in data presentation: types of reports, graphical representation, summary or detailed, presentation best practices. An assessment coordinator can be asked to provide a full report, several key bullet points, or an easy-to-read table. The information may be prepared for an oral presentation, a website, or a printed publication.

The timing of releasing assessment results needs to be considered, as well. Releasing key findings during the summer when many students and faculty are away can diminish the impact of the results and might cause concerns related to transparency.

What would you do? On behalf of the vice president, you completed a staff morale survey for all departments in your division. The results indicated very low morale in one particular department. The director of that department refused to share or use the results. Because of the state's open records laws, the information was released to a requestor—the results ended up on the front page of the local newspaper.

Items to consider include the following:

- Organizational structure and context, especially who has what type of power
- Identifying who (could be multiple people) has the ability to create change

Reflection Questions:

- What are the legal obligations to report and/or act on results?
- How might survey results be discussed without connecting them with job performance?

- Are there other champions for this issue on campus who could carry messages or take action?

Standard E: Exercise Personal and Professional Maturity, Good Judgment, and Critical Thinking Skills in the Reporting and Use of Assessment

Successful assessment coordinators know their own principles and apply them in the context in which they operate. Assessment coordinators should have excellent communication skills and be able to converse professionally, honestly, and in a manner that moves assessment forward while being sensitive to the potential impact of information shared.

Every institution also has traditions, explicit or implicit, and rules, written or unwritten, that impact assessment and the use of results. Assessment coordinators need to be astute about things that people at the institution are afraid or unwilling to criticize and question. On occasion, the student affairs assessment professional may recommend *not* doing an assessment at a particular time, especially if there is not an opportunity to effect change. Ideally, assessment coordinators are in a position to see the political context (or have a good relationship with a supervisor who can explain it and provide a buffer if needed). Because the assessment coordinators are not typically the people who make the actual programmatic changes, they need to understand the boundaries of their role while continuing to support the people who are the users of assessment.

Assessment coordinators need others' support to successfully do their jobs. They also need to know when to seek the counsel of others when they have questions or are unsure of the political environment and potential impact of collecting and sharing results. Trusted mentors and division leaders can provide assistance with dilemmas and can suggest courses of action. In these situations, assessment coordinators need to maintain high ethical standards related to the sharing and use of data.

Naïve assessment coordinators might think that data are objective, negating the need for an understanding and use of politics. In reality, while data may be objective, the assessment based on those data is not an objective process; decisions are made based on personal and professional knowledge, experiences, and philosophies. The most successful coordinators recognize their own subjectivity, the biases of people with whom they work, and the subjectivity of data interpretation and usage.

Similarly, assessment coordinators should be self-aware enough to recognize their weaknesses (whether a particular methodology or a particular topic) and develop ways to mediate them. For example, consider partnering with others who have a particular knowledge base or characteristics that would be beneficial to the understanding and use of information (e.g., a qualitative researcher to balance a quantitative researcher, a female to balance a male when assessing the campus climate for women).

What would you do? You have been asked to coordinate focus groups with student employees of a department. At first, the client wants to be present in the focus groups, but you convince her to let you do them alone. In the focus groups, the students express concern that their supervisor will be able to attribute comments to specific students in the analysis. There has been tension between the students and their supervisor.

Items to consider include the following:

- Organizational structure and context, especially who has what type of power
- Identifying where the results are reported and to what audiences

Reflection Questions:

- What are the ethical or legal obligations to report and/or act on results?
- What is the best way to report results while protecting confidentiality?
- How might results be discussed without connecting them with job performance?
- Who might need to get involved in conversations around the data/key findings before releasing them to the public or using them?

Standard F: Ability to Identify, Recognize, and Overcome Barriers to Performing Assessment and Incorporating Assessment Results Into Policy and Practice

Although staff members may appreciate having a full-time assessment coordinator with knowledge and skill, there may also be impediments in a successful transition. "Positons in student affairs, like those in most organizations, are also generally designed with a vertical organizational orientation" (Kuk, 2012b, p. 27). The assessment coordinator may be most effective collaborating horizontally. Although an external consultant can provide a fresh perspective, some staff members fear outsiders in their operations. Resolving this conflict takes leadership from top of the organization to set and reinforce expectations. In addition, it takes relationship building and patience on behalf of the assessment coordinator.

Change is difficult for some people. To support that change in the organization, Kuk (2012b) noted the following:

> Roles and responsibilities can be crafted and reinforced through rewards and other activities that promote changing the orientation of roles and responsibilities to be more lateral in their focus. Second, these changes can be reinforced by giving individuals greater decision making and resource sharing responsibilities that are collaborative in nature and more team-focused. (p. 29)

With a broader perspective, the assessment coordinator can bring people together with similar interests.

A common barrier relates to resources available to the assessment coordinator and the staff. This includes survey design software, data analysis software, project management resources, assessment reporting structures, and professional development. In order to integrate assessment practices into the day-to-day functions of organizations, these issues have to be resolved on institutional, divisional and unit levels. Leadership needs to be prepared to provide the infrastructure needed.

What would you do? You are in a newly created assessment coordinator position. The vice president has expressed a commitment to outcomes-based assessment and use of results. A director in the division has repeatedly and publically said he does not believe in assessment and does not allow his staff members to spend time on it (even though they see the value). The vice president is aware of this but will not take any actions to hold the department head accountable.

Items to consider include the following:

- Organizational structure and context, especially who has what type of power
- Accountability structure

Reflection Questions:

- Are the assessment coordinator and director being supervised by the same person? Different people? How does that alter the situation?
- How does one work with an individual who is hesitant to participate in assessment in a manner that builds confidence and shows the rewards? What are some alternative ways?
- What might be one small step to take to try to move the conversation forward?

Recommendations

Assessment coordinators need to have a clear sense of their own assessment beliefs and values, as well as an understanding of professional association and institution ethical standards. Consulting with colleagues and reflecting on political and ethical case studies can guide that process. It is helpful to do this on a regular basis as contexts change.

Assessment coordinators must have open and frequent communication with their supervisors about the political climate, ethical standards, and expectations. The supervisors may have a better sense of the environment, current issues, and key players in decisions in order to provide a buffer if needed. Refrain from doing a study no one wants, know who are supporters and detractors, and involve stakeholders early.

Assessment coordinators need to be keen observers of the political and decision-making environment. Knowing who has the ability to make change is key, as is understanding how people will be affected by results.

Because assessment may cause fear for some staff, it is necessary for assessment coordinators to build coalitions. Especially for new positions and new people in the assessment coordinator position, building positive relationships in the beginning may be just as important as the assessment process itself. Creating partnerships can assuage the fear and turn the critics into supporters.

References

American College Personnel Association. (2006). *Assessment skills and knowledge: Content standards for student affairs practitioners and scholars (ASK)*. Washington, DC: ACPA.

Bresciani, M. J. (2012). Changing roles and responsibilities in student affairs research and assessment. In A. Tull & L. Kuk (Eds.), *New realities in the management of student affairs: Emerging specialist roles and structures for changing times* (pp. 114–122). Sterling, VA: Stylus.

Carreon, J. (2011). A commitment to serving our changing communities. In G. J. Dungy & S. E. Ellis (Eds.), *Exceptional senior student affairs administrators: Strategies and competencies for success* (pp. 145–152). Washington, DC: NASPA.

Cavins-Tull, K. (2012). Facilitating organizational change to incorporate specialist roles and matrix structures in student affairs organizations. In A. Tull & L. Kuk (Eds.), *New realities in the management of student affairs: Emerging specialist roles and structures for changing times* (pp. 129–148). Sterling, VA: Stylus.

Kuk, L. (2012a). The changing nature of student affairs. In A. Tull & L. Kuk (Eds.), *New realities in the management of student affairs: Emerging specialist roles and structures for changing times* (pp. 3–12). Sterling, VA: Stylus.

Kuk, L. (2012b). The context for using specialist roles and matrix structures in student affairs organizations. In A. Tull & L. Kuk (Eds.), *New realities in the management of student affairs: Emerging specialist roles and structures for changing times* (pp. 13–33). Sterling, VA: Stylus.

Lis Dean, K. (2013). Politics in assessment. In D. M. Timm, J. D. Barham, K. McKinney, & A. R. Knerr (Eds.), *Assessment in practice: A companion guide to the ASK standards* (pp. 63–72). Washington, DC: ACPA.

Schuh, J. H., & Upcraft, M. L. (2000). Assessment politics. *About Campus, 5*(4), 14–21.

Timm, D. M., Barham, J. D., McKinney, K., & Knerr, A. R. (2013). *Assessment in practice: A companion guide to the ASK standards*. Washington, DC: ACPA.

Upcraft, M. L., & Schuh, J. H. (2002). Assessment vs. research: Why we should care about the difference. *About Campus, 7*(1), 16–20.

10 Tenet Ten: "Other Duties as Assigned"

Kimberly Yousey-Elsener
Erin M. Bentrim

IN ADDITION to the official position description and professional responsibilities, those in assessment coordinator roles have noticed that the position tends to be one that receives many "other duties as assigned." The nature of the position seems to lend itself to this phenomenon for numerous reasons, including the following:.

- **Structural organization.** Assessment coordinators are usually positioned structurally in an organization where they have the unique perspective of knowing/seeing the "big picture" at the vice president level while also having a sense of the "small picture" in each unit.
- **Evolving nature and flexibility.** Because of the nature of assessment work, assessment coordinators are often technology-friendly people who are willing to test and implement new technologies unrelated to assessment work.
- **Work ethic and skills.** Assessment coordinators are often seen as people who can get the job done. People in this type of position tend to be organized with exceptional time management skills. They are able to pull together large-scale projects and have excellent written and verbal capabilities.
- **Need for data.** Committees and other working groups often request the "data person" as a committee member.
- **Physical location.** With office space physically located within a vice presidential or other larger suite, assessment coordinators are physically present and within eyesight. This results in being assigned projects that do not have a natural fit in any other unit.

148

There are many advantages to some of these other duties; there are also challenges. Sometimes the other duties overpower the assessment work, leaving little time and capacity to do the things necessary to move assessment forward and do the real work for which one was hired. Other times it leaves one wondering, "Why do I have a PhD (or insert any other descriptor)?" If nothing else, sharing the "war stories" with other assessment professionals tends to make for humorous storytelling at conferences and other gatherings.

No matter what the duty or the effect it has on the overall assessment work, this chapter uses examples from professionals around the United States to demonstrate some of the many "other duties" assessment coordinators have encountered. Given the lack of research on this topic, the bulk of this chapter is based on informal conversations and a short survey sent to the members of the Student Affairs Assessment Leaders (SAAL) electronic mailing list. The specific names and titles of the people who contributed these examples have been left off to protect anonymity and reputations, but these examples are real. As is often said in residence life and other circles, you can't make this stuff up!

In addition, this chapter explores some of the benefits of doing these "other duties" and ends with the editors' best advice for avoiding mission creep and undue focus on other duties that can take away from the core work of assessment. Ultimately, it is important to note that even the most unrelated duties can be used as an opportunity to move assessment efforts forward and to keep a sense of humor at the end of the day.

Other Duties Somewhat Related to the Job

This first category involves fellow assessment coordinators describing other duties that could concievably fit with their job but could be considered a stretch of the job description, as well. These other duties include things like the following:

- Being "proofreader-in-chief" for major (and sometimes minor) documents coming from the vice president's or other offices.

- Being the "student affairs rep" on university committees that have nothing to do with being an assessment professional, and being given overwhelming amounts of committee work in general. As one SAAL member stated, "I often get brought into committee work to assist with an assessment piece and then end up continuing to work on the committee." (anonymous, personal communication, July 22, 2014)
- Being the data analyzer, report creator, or survey designer for units outside of student affairs with little say in how the data are collected or used.
- Managing databases or cross-referencing information from different systems on campus. This is sometimes related to student affairs work but sometimes for offices beyond the division.
- Taking notes at cabinet and other leadership or committee meetings.
- Evaluating new technology purchases and developing proposals for what should be purchase/implemented.
- Assisting with regional conference committees and/or evaluations even though one is not even a member of that organization.
- Serving on and chairing search committees.
- Assisting with developing, implementing, conducting, and organizing the data from employee performance evaluation processes.
- Being a keynote speaker at an event that may or may not be related to assessment.
- Serving as the vice president's or other associate vice presidents' administrative assistant.
- Leading division-level initiatives such as strategic planning, professional development, book clubs, annual budget reviews, and so on.

As seen from these examples, the other duties related to assessment work can come in different forms and are frequently affected by the coordinator's physical office location, structural position in the organization, or perceived skill set. (*Perceived* is the key term here; one survey participant mentioned that his/her family and friends find it humorous that he/she is seen as a "technology expert" at work and yet doesn't own a smartphone or tablet and rarely works with a computer when home.)

Other Duties Not Related to Assessment Work

Assessment coordinators also recounted tasks and projects that were not even remotely related to their job description or work in assessment. Some tasks bordered on the unbelievable. The following are a few examples that SAAL members sent in. Please enjoy, and thank you to all who submitted these examples.

- Coordinating and/or serving on the planning team for annual division-wide social events like holiday parties, summer BBQs, and happy hour gatherings. One person remembered designing and assembling centerpieces for an event each year—hot glue guns and all! Another shared walking around campus with the president's wife looking for mistletoe in the trees to be used at a holiday party.
- Designing/creating homegrown social media and other websites.
- Teaching freshmen seminar courses.
- Being the official golf cart driver, car unloader, parent greeter, welcome tent volunteer, scooper at the ice cream social, early arrival coordinator, and so on, for opening weekend/move-in.
- Being in charge of refreshments, including bringing the vice president coffee or ordering catering for larger gatherings.
- Volunteering at large-scale events such as commencement and other weekend programs.
- Serving in interim roles when a position was temporarily vacant. Examples include chief judicial officer, registrar, student involvement/leadership director, sexual assault advocate, and parent liaison or parent orientation leader. Other members were assigned on-call duties and took on additional jobs to fill in for people on long-term absences such as maternity leave.
- Being the website developer or primary web contact for the division.

- Being invited to consult for a committee (division or university) on an assessment-related issue only to end up becoming a permanent member of a committee that had no relation to assessment. One person reported spending two days making candy bags for university employees as a member of a committee for which the person was initially asked to briefly consult.
- Organizing volunteers for special events such as presidential debates (yes, *the* president of the United States), presidential visits, state and local government speeches, and events on campus.
- Providing manual labor, including setting up tables at events, putting stickers on giveaways, being a human directional sign at events, and so on.

As you can see, assessment coordinators should be prepared to be asked to assist with anything and everything, depending on their *perceived* skill set.

Tangible Benefits

When asking assessment coordinators about some of their "other duties," there was a collective sense of humor, frustration, and accomplishment. The challenges of some of the duties were obvious: Why am I doing this? How can I get my "real" work done when I have all this extra stuff? Nevertheless, no matter what the duty and how related or unrelated to assessment work, everyone who participated in the survey described some tangible benefits to participating in these duties. One person summed up the top benefits best:

> I see two major benefits. First, it gives me exposure to other areas, operations, and projects beyond my immediate world. Such deviations from standard projects can be a breath of fresh air. Second, it can lead to increased collaboration with faculty, staff, and/or students at the institution (and beyond!). It's always great to increase your network and never hurts to promote assessment to other folks—even if you're only doing so by explaining your role/the area you work in. (anonymous, personal communication, July 22, 2014)

The first benefit was building rapport, including making connections, building networks, and ultimately ensuring future support for assessment work. Assessment coordinators are usually in the position of needing people to get assessment done but having no real power or authority to make someone do assessment. For this reason, having faculty and staff members view the assessment coordinator as helpful and a team player goes a long way in getting assessment work accomplished. Whether it's getting to know someone while driving a golf cart, bonding over making holiday centerpieces, helping someone with a data analysis project, or being the person known for providing the team's favorite doughnut holes, out-of-the-box teamwork builds goodwill and good favor among people who are needed to make assessment successful.

The second commonly cited benefit was gaining access to information and knowledge. All those committees and working groups that seem unrelated to assessment work provide the assessment coordinator with knowledge of what is happening on campus, what issues are occurring, and understanding challenges and successes. This is especially important in institutions that are siloed or in departments that are highly autonomous and where information sharing does not regularly occur. This information is useful when planning what data need to be collected, where data need to be shared, and how to find new sources for data and information. In addition, it provides perspective on the work that others are doing.

A third benefit many people cited was exposure to units and areas outside student affairs. Politically speaking, it is great to be seen as an expert on campus. Indeed, being able to participate in other duties that involve skill sets such as data analysis, effective written communication, and so on, is a highly valued capability. While working on strategic planning, writing self-studies, guiding data collection outside student affairs, and so on may sometimes divert from other projects, it is good to remember that ultimately connections are being made and reputations built, and one never knows where that may lead.

A fourth benefit mentioned was learning new technology. Like it or not, assessment work involves using technology to make the process itself more efficient. Being asked to consult or evaluate the purchasing of new technology or updating current technology expands the assessment coordinator's knowledge of what is available for future assessment endeavors and stretches a skill set. Whether it is a new student information system, early-alert retention system, student involvement platform, strategic planning system, e-portfolio, or instructional platform, all of these technologies have a data component and can serve as rich sources of information for an assessment coordinator. Being involved in evaluating, implementing, or improving these systems gives a new perspective, makes connections with the people managing the technology, and sets the coordinator up for successful use of these technologies in the future.

Advice Related to Other Duties

This chapter, and the data collected for it, are presented in a good-natured fashion and with a sense of humor, but the reality is that everyone serving as a student affairs assessment coordinator has experienced an "other duty." Although the benefits are real, the challenges can be great and mission creep is a real danger when it comes to these types of assignments. To prevent a complete change in job description, here is some advice to keep in mind:

- Learn how to empower yourself to say "no" and diplomatically explain why.
- Be aware of when your "downtime" is as well as when the "peak times" are for other units, and be willing to take one for the team every now and then. While that golf cart gig on move-in day might seem like a wasted day, the relationships that are built can be priceless.
- Do not be afraid to ask to be removed from a committee if the work is getting time-consuming and is no longer related to assessment.
- Try to establish an honest relationship with your supervisor so he or she can help you maintain balance. If that relationship is not there, it may be time to consider other options.
- Keep an eye on the political benefits of participating in something and balance it with the cost of time and effort.
- Be honest about how long data projects and reports can take. Colleagues often assume that a magic button can be pushed and—"poof!"—out come data. One person mentioned that they were referred as the person who "poofs" data projects into reports.

As a newly appointed assessment coordinator, it is important to take note of this advice and these examples. Balancing the demand for time and competing priorities is one of the greatest challenges in this role. Ascertaining the benefits and pitfalls associated with becoming involved in other duties can help prioritize commitments and additional responsibilities.

Editors and Contributors

Editors

Kimberly Yousey-Elsener is the director of assessment and evaluation for University Life and Services at the University of Buffalo. In addition, she serves as associate editor for internal publications for ACPA and on the faculty for the College Student Personnel Administration program at Canisius College. She recently published *Successful Assessment in Student Affairs: A How-To Guide* and *Data Collection and Reporting* with PaperClip Communications. Her experience in higher education includes teaching at the undergraduate and graduate levels, residence life, academic advising/support, service-learning, student activities, and assessment, as well as serving as an assessment consultant for Campus Labs. She received a doctorate from New York University in higher education administration and policy, a master's degree from Kent State University in college student personnel administration, and a bachelor's of music education from Baldwin-Wallace College.

Erin M. Bentrim is a visiting assistant professor of psychology at Wingate University. She is also a consultant who specializes in student assessment and strategic planning. Over the past 23 years, Bentrim has served in a variety of positions in higher education administration, including assistant dean of students, interim director of academic assessment, and the director of institutional research and effectiveness. In addition, Bentrim has held faculty appointments at the undergraduate and graduate levels. She has led several strategic planning initiatives in her local community and served as an assessment consultant for multiple campuses. She was the national cochair of the NASPA Assessment, Evaluation, and Research Knowledge Community from 2009 to 2011 and is a founding member of the Student Affairs Assessment Leaders. She holds a PhD in educational psychology and research and an MEd in student personnel services from the University of South Carolina and a BA in English from Wofford College.

Gavin W. Henning is a college student educator with a reputation as a coordinator, collaborator, and catalyst for educational change. He has more than 20 years of higher education experience that includes faculty, student affairs assessment, institutional research, and residence life. As associate professor and program director at New England College in New Hampshire, Henning coordinates the master's of higher education administration and doctorate of education programs. He has served as president of ACPA—College Student Educators International as well as on the board of directors and executive committee of the Council for the Advancement of Standards in Higher Education (CAS). Henning holds a doctor of philosophy degree in education leadership and policy studies and a master of arts degree in sociology, both from the University of New Hampshire, as well as a master of arts degree in college and university administration and a bachelor of science degree in psychology and sociology from Michigan State University.

Contributors

Robert W. Aaron serves as executive director of the Center for the Study of Student Life (CSSL) at The Ohio State University. In this position he directs research, assessment, and policy planning efforts related to students who interact with all departments in the Office of Student Life. Aaron joined the CSSL staff in 2014 after serving as director of student affairs assessment and planning at Indiana University–Purdue University Indianapolis. Previously, he worked for the National Survey of Student Engagement as a project associate and later as client services manager. He has also worked in student affairs at Virginia Commonwealth University with positions in the first-year experience, fraternity and sorority life, and student activities. He earned a PhD in higher education from Indiana University, an MA in higher education and student affairs from The Ohio State University, and a BA in music from University of Rochester.

Dan Bureau is the special assistant to the vice president for student affairs and director of student affairs learning and assessment at the University of Memphis. In his 19-year career in student affairs, he has worked in a range of functional areas, including fraternity/sorority life and leadership programs prior to his work with assessment and planning. He serves on the board of directors for the Council for the Advancement of Standards in Higher Education (CAS) and has held leadership roles in a range of higher education organizations. He has presented at numerous conferences and published in association journals and magazines.

Michael Christakis is vice president for student success and public service professor at the University at Albany. In this role, Christakis serves as the university's chief student affairs officer and provides leadership and vision in administering a comprehensive student affairs program that promotes the academic achievement and personal development of all students and fosters collaborative relationships among students, faculty, staff, and the community. Known nationally for his work in student affairs assessment, Christakis led efforts to develop a comprehensive assessment program for student success prior to the university's reaccreditation in 2010 and is credited with developing the "Student Learning Project," the university's cocurricular student learning outcomes framework, for which he received the 2012 NASPA Assessment, Evaluation, and Research Knowledge Community Innovation Award. Christakis earned his BA in political science and history from Alfred University and his MPP and PhD from the University at Albany's Rockefeller College of Public Affairs and Policy.

James R. Doyle has worked in student affairs for 48 years. He retired from DePaul University in 2012 after serving as vice president for student affairs for 30 years. In 2002, as the chief student affairs officer at DePaul, he called upon colleagues in the fields of institutional research and academic affairs to assist the division in developing a division-wide assessment model, reflective of the institution's approach to assessment. Over the next 14 years Doyle dedicated personnel and resources to support assessment across the division. After retiring from DePaul, Doyle spent two years in Dublin, Ireland, working at All Hallows College as dean of academic affairs and student engagement. Prior to his work at DePaul, Doyle worked at Creighton University for 10 years, spending 5 years as vice president of student affairs, and also worked at Loyola University–Chicago, Marquette University, and the University of San Diego. He has taught in DePaul's higher education program and continues to work in higher education consulting.

Becki Elkins is registrar and director of institutional research and assessment at Cornell College in Mount Vernon, Iowa. She holds a doctorate in student affairs administration and research from the University of Iowa, a master's degree from Iowa State University, and a bachelor's degree from the University of Kansas. She has more than 20 years of experience in higher education. Elkins has held professional roles in residence life, women's and LGBT centers, institutional research, assessment, and registrar's office. Her publications address topics such as student affairs assessment, accreditation, student and academic affairs partnerships, multicultural initiatives, and graduate student needs. Her professional interests include assessment of student learning, social justice, qualitative research methods, and student success. She is currently an adjunct faculty member in the higher education student affairs program at the University of Iowa. In her free time, Elkins enjoys biking, spending time with her family, reading, and writing.

Ted Elling is the associate vice chancellor for student affairs for research and systems development at the University of North Carolina at Charlotte. His current responsibilities include coordinating research, assessment, and information technology efforts for the division. He also serves as the senior project manager of various division- and university-wide initiatives. He received his EdD in higher and adult education from Columbia University with an emphasis in student personnel administration. His research interests include data integration to enable assessment and program evaluation in addition to new student retention and graduation rate issues. He has published in the areas of minority student retention, assessment in student affairs, information technology, data integration, and the influence of work on college student development, and he is a past national cochair of the NASPA Assessment, Evaluation, and Research Knowledge Community and past chair of the Student Affairs Assessment Leaders organization.

Justin Keen is the director of assessment and planning for the student development division at University of Dayton where he also completed his master's in college student personnel. Keen's professional interests center on authentic assessment in student affairs and the role of reflective practice in organizational improvement. He is currently pursuing a doctorate in educational leadership.

Ellen S. Meents-DeCaigny is assistant vice president for student affairs at DePaul University where she oversees divisional initiatives related to assessment, research, strategic planning, communications, information management, budget, and human resources. She earned her PhD in higher education from Loyola University Chicago, her MA in counseling and college student development from the University of Maryland, and her BA in speech communications from Drake University. Meents-DeCaigny served as cochair of the NASPA National Assessment, Evaluation, and Research Knowledge Community from 2010 to 2013 and currently serves as a member of the NASPA Professional Standards Division. In addition to presenting on the topic of assessment at various regional and national conferences, she has served as a faculty member for Academic Impressions' Assessment Institute and has served as a consultant to various institutions and organizations regarding assessment. She has also coauthored five chapters on assessment.

Darby Roberts is the director of student life studies at Texas A&M University, which serves the division of student affairs and the division of student organizations for their comprehensive assessment needs. She also teaches in the student affairs administration in higher education master's program. Roberts has served as cochair for NASPA's Assessment, Evaluation, and Research Knowledge Community and was a founding member of Student Affairs Assessment Leaders. Her interest in assessing cocurricular student learning led to *Learning Is Not a Sprint: Assessing and Documenting Student Leader Learning in Cocurricular Involvement* (Washington, DC: NASPA, 2012). She frequently presents, consults, and writes about student affairs assessment. Before becoming a full-time assessment professional in 1998, Roberts worked in residence life and advised student organizations.

Larry D. Roper is a professor in the School of Language, Culture, and Society and coordinator of the College Student Services Administration program and the undergraduate social justice minor at Oregon State University. He served as vice provost for student affairs from 1995–2014. He has degrees from Heidelberg University, Bowling Green State University, and the University of Maryland. He has held numerous positions in student affairs, including director of housing, associate dean of students, coordinator of multicultural affairs, and vice president for student affairs/dean of students. Roper currently serves as a commissioner with the State of Oregon's Higher Education Coordinating Commission and as chair of the NASPA Faculty Fellows. He served four years as editor and six years as a commissioner with the Northwest Commission on Colleges and Universities.

Vicki L. Wise is the associate director for teaching, learning, and assessment at Western Governors University. Wise's passion is helping faculty and staff design and assess programs and services that facilitate student learning and development. She has also served as director for assessment and research at Portland State University in student affairs. Prior to her position at Portland State University, she held the positions of director of assessment and evaluation for the College of Education, assistant director for institutional research, and assistant professor/research administrator in the Center for Assessment and Research Studies, all at James Madison University. She earned her PhD in psychological and cultural studies and her MA in educational psychology at the University of Nebraska.

Index

why assessment matters and how to implement assessment practice so that inquiry becomes a priority, deeply embedded into the daily work of all who believe in and contribute to student success.

It shares various ways to evaluate implementation of student success theory and practice in a manner that leads to improving relevant outcomes. Upon reading, you will likely gain ideas to cultivate a culture of inquiry along with important means to communicate results to stakeholders and garner their feedback for prioritizing recommendations. This book provides a 'how to' in making assessment an integral practice of the student affairs profession.

It is my hope that the leaders (read: all of you) who are reading this book are the leaders who have that kind of courage—the courage to hold space for transformation to occur. If so, I invite you to read this book and fully engage in the lessons colleagues share. Explore how the ideas presented in these pages may be adapted and taken up within your organization. Then, collaboratively execute and enjoy the fruits of your investment in meaningful inquiry."

—*Marilee J. Bresciani Ludvik, Professor, Postsecondary Education, San Diego State University*

Sty/us

22883 Quicksilver Drive
Sterling, VA 20166-2102   Subscribe to our e-mail alerts: www.Styluspub.com

to the richness of undergraduate life. What's more, institutional illustrations and examples add robustness to this book through detailed treatment of central topics in outcomes assessment."

"I wish this guide had been available six years ago when we began our learning outcomes assessment journey. The critical elements of outcomes-based assessment are clearly articulated with application at both the program and system levels. The book is practical, concise, and convincing. The criticalness of outcomes-based assessment as an essential element of the student learning experience is clearly communicated. I can't wait to get the guide into the hands of our student affairs managers. *Demonstrating Student Success* takes the intimidation factor out of the critically important task of outcomes-based assessment. The concepts and best practices are presented with the student affairs practitioner in mind with ready-to-use approaches and plans."

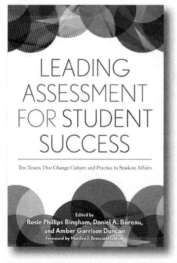

Leading Assessment for Student Success

Ten Tenets That Change Culture and Practice in Student Affairs

Edited by Rosie Phillips Bingham, Daniel A. Bureau, and Amber Garrison Duncan

Foreword by Marilee J. Bresciani Ludvik

"This book explains how to tell the story of assessment while engaging each student affairs team member on your campus, whether it is the senior student affairs officer or a frontline professional. Each chapter builds on the previous, making the case for

(Continues on preceding page)

Also available from Stylus

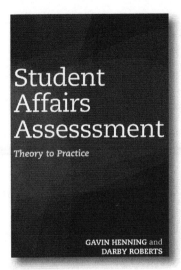

Student Affairs Assessment

Theory to Practice

Gavin W. Henning and Darby Roberts

Foreword by Marilee J. Bresciani Ludvik

This book is intended as both a text for student affairs and higher education master's programs and a practical guide for early career staff who have had little formal preparation in assessment. It can be used for self-study or in professional development workshops. For divisions, departments, or units getting started with assessment, the discussion questions at the end of the chapters can engage staff in the process of developing an effective assessment culture.

This book provides a thorough introduction to all aspects of assessment, assuming no prior knowledge, and is illustrated throughout with examples of application in student affairs settings.

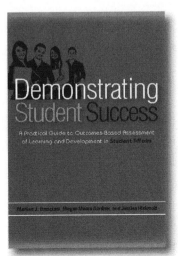

Demonstrating Student Success

A Practical Guide to Outcomes-Based Assessment of Learning and Development in Student Affairs

Marilee J. Bresciani, Megan Moore Gardner, and Jessica Hickmott

"This volume is a wonderful addition to existing resources on assessment in student affairs. Its value is in its focus on a crucial form of assessment: demonstrating how student experiences contribute

(Continues on preceding page)